The Marriage Grit

an Anthology

The Marriage Grit

Happie Face Publishing Company

Copyright © 2020 All rights reserved.

ISBN: 978-0-9994726-7-5

MARRIAGE GRIT

An internalized resilience; coupled with grave desire, fueled by individualized determination, perseverance, intentional love, and endurance for the collaborative union of one.

Rob and Tawana Peterson

ABOUT THE MARRIAGE GRIT

In every moment together, and even in our moments apart, we develop key levels of expertise, thus preparing us as a couple for the next dimension of our union. These various levels of expertise are created through thousands and thousands of experiences, which can only be defined as *marriage*.

While many would consider marriage as "work," we have embarked on a journey to redefine not only the ideology of marriage, but to redefine the worldview of such. Consider your personal discussions; think about the conversations had with friends in the barbershop, beauty salon, or even your place or worship. We have all been faced with the important question, "How's marriage?" Although the question is not rhetorical, the response remains the same: marriage is work! While a specific level of effort is involved, the concept of mastering wedlock should be an enjoyable journey, til' death do we part. The work involved in the relationship has more to do with necessary individual adjustments for the benefit of the union. We each bring all sorts of personal conditions into the relationship. As such, our individual attitudes, selfish ways or personal agendas must be addressed in order to become "one." Sorting through all the individual junk is the most labor-intensive aspect of marriage. However, it only becomes work because this level of change is not only frustrating, but it is also unnatural.

The purpose of The Marriage Grit is to support couples through the process of "Mastering Wedlock." Through the various vicissitudes of marriage, each one must be encountered together. Doing so provides the collaborative effort necessary to achieve greatness, rather than venturing through the wilderness of life, searching for individual answers. In the chapters of this book, you will find couples that have made the decision to capitalize on the vows of marriage. From beginning to end, each statement considers our daily encounters as couples. Just as the days, months and years progress, each vow builds upon the other. It is to our benefit to revisit where we first began in order to capitalize on the experiences shared to make our unions strong examples of marriage grit.

The stories in the text are real. The participants in this book share the same level of optimism of The Marriage Grit. That the person holding this book deserves transparency and truth from a first-person perspective. This book is not for any form of entertainment, but rather a call to action with the hopes that you as the reader will know that your individual experiences are not foreign or strange. You should know that collectively, you have the ability to decide to progress forward in the mastery of wedlock together as one couple.

HOW TO READ THIS BOOK

This book is divided into two parts – the wives' perspective and husbands' perspective. To read the wives' points of view, read from the front towards the middle. To read the husbands' points of view, read from the middle to the back. Refer to wives' content page in the front and the husbands' content page in the middle (pg. 128) to find your way.

AUTHORS
Wives (in alphabetical order)

Monique Bailey
Sandra Bailey
Mary Ernestine Chance, MDiv
Tanya Moorehead-Cooley, Ph.D.
Patricia D. Harris
Kiara Moore, LPCMH
Tawana M. Peterson
Candice Resto
Christina Watlington, Ph.D.

CONTENTS
Wives' Side

1	For Better or Worse	12
2	Marriage & Ministry	22
3	In Sickness & In Health	36
4	Blended Families	48
5	Marriage & Infertility	62
6	Interracial Marriage	72
7	Supporting Your Spouse's Dreams	82
8	Marriage & Longevity	94
***	*Poems (appear before every chapter)*	

We stood face to face, hand in hand and professed our love to the end.
We knew there would be ups and downs
But our promise to one another keeps us on solid ground.
And while we continue to grow day by day
Our worse becomes better and together we stay.

● *Patricia D. Harris*

For Better or Worse

1

For Better or For Worse
Tawana M. Peterson

For better or for worse. What does that really mean and is it a commitment that we will truly stand on for the rest of our lives? Do we mean it when we say it? Have we given the time to think about what that could mean? Are we strong enough to withstand the austerity that life may bring, especially after riding on a cloud, no matter what number it was?

Test and trials will come, even when two lovers are the best of friends. As the song says, "Can you stand the rain?" I'm sure after reading that line, you probably heard the song playing in your mind. You may have even snapped your fingers and swayed from side to side. The R&B group, New Edition, stamped an everlasting love song in the hearts of all that lived in that era, but be honest, when you fell in love, did you think about how or if you would be able or willing to go from better to worse not knowing when or if the better would return? I'm sure many of us have said, "I'm not even going to claim that!" and rightfully so. That is what we ought to say. It's called positive affirmation.

When we got married, like salvation, no one said that the road would be easy. The decision to uphold morals, follow your heart, or commit to the relationship is daunting when adding another person into the picture. However, when you have a partner with the same sagacity as you, you can expect just as much or more bliss and ecstasy as you may expect catastrophe and misadventure. Okay, so why did I get married? I can do bad all by myself, right? Wrong! Even misery loves company.

The Bible says, "It is not good for the man to be alone," (Genesis 2:18). You might think, "Cool, but what does that have to do with me? I'm a woman…"

Well woman, you were created to be a helpmeet – that is, when you decided to get married. Now, I know that we as women are gifted and talented to be "every woman" that our man needs. On top of that, we are graced with the wit to be a boss, Ms. Independent. We can wear many hats and stun the onlookers while doing so and we can create something out of nothing (ladies, don't try to create your man. That's for another book!). However, as a wife, once we've said, "I do," it is our responsibility to use our gifts and talents, boss tendencies, and independence to be the best helpmeet we can be and get through the better or worse times.

I know many will say, "I'm not taking care of no man!" and I get it; he's the provider and the head of household and we should not try to switch roles, even if for a season or second, he's at home and you're working your business or a 9-to-5 job. He is still the head. Does he lose reign or value within your heart and mind should this hinge arise? Does your eye suddenly have dual vision resulting from this unforeseen circumstance that is taking over 120 days to change? Does your kind words and level of affection diminish because deep inside you're experiencing a bit of direct or indirect frustration? In your moments of despair, what is your go-to for change? Let's look at it from another view. Most of us were guilty of that pre-wedding "fit kick," where we work out intensely to make sure we present our best selves on that day. Prior to that, we were consistently keeping our bodies, hair, nails, and dress game up to par to be eye candy for a brother or just for our own self-gratification. However, much like the "Freshman 15" scenario, after the wedding, life or children came along and made some changes pile on to our bottle shapes or not having the convenience of time for putting stuff on like we used to. None of these things are detrimental, but they could cause concern or distaste to the one whose eyes you caught. He may never say a word, or he may say, "I love you just the way you are," but I want to pose this question. How do you keep the bliss and the ecstasy present when change comes to challenge you? From a wife's perspective, what do you do when the worst is you?

No matter what the scenario may be, self-reflection is the key to restoration of any situation. Pray, meditate, and mediate. These serve as bridges between experience and learning. Experience the episode, positively react to it, and gain insight from it. Don't play the blame game. Think of how you can help empower and encourage your man to get back to his rightful place. Consider how you can evolve into a greater form of you.

We believe that trouble doesn't last. Trials come to make

you stronger than what you were before the heavy weights increased. When you push past that pain and discomfort, you can lift those weights with the power perpetuated within. There will be times when you must dig way down and pull out what you never believed existed. It's by having the faith to believe that there is something more to it than what you currently see. By faith, you are more powerful than the obstacle standing in your way. By faith, you can speak things into existence. By faith, every negative thing that once was no longer, is. Faith is believing, believing is seeing, and seeing is acknowledging what you perceive. How do you perceive the outcome of your circumstances? Although a challenge comes, does that mean you're to throw in the towel and decide that your marriage is not for you? I believe not.

"If we had no winter, the spring would not be so pleasant; if we did not sometimes taste of adversity, prosperity would not be so welcome."
– Anne Bradstreet

Twenty-three years of marriage is no walk in the park. It is a feat that is hard to find for couples that are in their 40s. As a young wife, I certainly didn't have any answers. All I knew was that a young man sought for me and loved me for who I was. He gave me every reason to be a better me and to shine like the diamond he found. Not willing to lose the opportunity to find this sincere love from a man who had a true love for God, I became like Ruth and followed the guidance and instruction of my Naomi. Wisdom comes when you humble yourself and receive the lessons that arise from the challenge we face.

The best thing that Robert and I did was decide to get married. The worst part of the decision was the fact that we were placed in a canoe together, depending on each other to survive. The best thing that we did was always have each other's back and to row the boat together and alternatively as needed. The worst thing about that was that we felt each other's pain. The best thing about allowing vulnerability to step in was that it enabled us to see the worst things we faced as light afflictions that don't compare to the glorious times shared. The worst thing we've experienced were setbacks, misunderstandings, disagreements, and unforeseen losses. The best things that we experienced were love, joy, peace, patience, kindness, goodness, faithfulness, gentleness and self-control.

When you measure the best and worst factors of your marriage, you find where the value lies. It's from there that you do one of two things; keep doing what you do or build to make it better. We win together – that is our motto and we both decided back in 1994, before we said, "I do," that we weren't "goin' nowhere." Translation: "You're all that I want, all that I need, and all that I hoped for; the only way that this relationship ends is if you leave." Now, because there was no physical or mental danger involved, these words were and are alright with me.

A recent quote from a very intelligent writer, Dr. Heather Tucker, stated, "*We may not have it all together, but together we have it all.*" Robert and I certainly did not have it all figured out when we exchanged our vows, after the honeymoon, or after child number three, four or five. However, we knew that together, we had all that we would ever need to make it through what life presented to us. It's through having a determined and prayed-up mindset that leads you towards your desired destiny. You must want it, and with God, you can have it! Most marriages don't work out because someone didn't want it. If you are reading this chapter and you are not married but are considering it, be sure that both of you want the same things within your relationship. For better or worse, you must remain true to your individuality, but agree collectively on what you want your marriage to look like. Wives, whether you've been married for four days, four years, forty-four years or more, it's up to you to have that made up mind to consider the needs of your marriage and the same is true for your husband.

Self-reflection comes first, because while we are aiming to be a helpmeet, we must help ourselves first. We cannot help our husbands if we are not whole and vice versa. No matter what state you find yourself in, for better or worse indicates that you are making a conscious decision to maintain your marriage status. You are making a conscious decision to put your best heels on and walk it out together. We talk about having the faith to visualize before things materialize. You'll find out that you can make it through anything when you determine that your marriage will win, for better or for worse!

Tawana Peterson

Before there was US, there was You and there was Me.
Worlds so far apart, there was no way that it could be.
But together we are here, serving, loving, and encouraging our community.
We are so grateful for this life changing opportunity.

● *Patricia D. Harris*

Marriage & Ministry

2

Marriage & Ministry
Monique Bailey

I initially gave my life to Christ at the age of 15, just a year after I met who I believed was my soulmate, Blaine. The joy I had was so remarkable and refreshing that I wanted everyone I knew to be able to experience that same joy. Every chance I got, I called Blaine and told him about God. He started to dodge my calls because he knew God would be the focus, but I think he loved me more than he disliked the conversations because he eventually gave in.

I realized that this guy had some invisible strings that were pulling at my heart. I was smitten by him. His hold on me was so obvious that my grandmother, who was my pastor, told me to stop talking to him so much because I was not "spiritually strong" enough to combat the temptation.

I ignored the warning and continued to sneak and talk to him and before long, I backslide. Initially, I was okay with the decision that I made to be with him because he was the first guy that made me feel special. In the summer, he would take me to the park to feed the ducks and in the winter, we would play in the snow. For the first time in my life, I experienced what true love was. We spent a lot of our time together and when we were apart, we would talk on the phone for hours.

I was 17 when my mom let me take her car to go see Blaine. We went out to a club in Philadelphia. I was dancing, having a great time when suddenly the thought of me going to hell came to me and I immediately felt condemned. As we headed back to Chester, I got physically sick. Blaine had to pull the car over because I started to vomit. I didn't eat or drink anything out of the ordinary that would have made me ill, so I took it as a sign that I needed to get my life right.

Not long after that night, I had a talk with Blaine. I told

him I needed to get myself together which meant that we could no longer be together. Though we were heartbroken, he said he would rather not be with me and I be happy than to be with me and I be unhappy.

I started attending church regularly again and repented. When I thought about how much I loved Blaine, the thought of his soul being lost and him going to hell was something I couldn't bear, so I made it my mission to continue to tell him about Christ and even invited him to church. A few months later, he came to church with me and after about two months, he sought after God for himself.

At 22, I married the love of my life. Two to three years went by and my husband was called into the ministry as a minister. It was just like God to call me too. We prayed, praised, and worshipped together. We had two children that we brought up in the church and we modeled what serving God looked like for them.

After about 11 years, I began to feel spiritually drained. Someone that abused me in my early teenage years joined the same church we attended and the recognition he was getting for being so "wonderful" really began to overwhelm me. Bishops and pastors praised him so much for always being a help to them and I couldn't stomach it. Though I prayed and fasted, it was still too much for me to bear. I was holding on to that secret to the point where it was eating away at me like a cancer.

Little by little, I began to hate going to church, not only because I had to face my abuser but because my growth was stagnant. I would be on my way to church, crying my eyeballs out because I felt like no one would understand how I felt. I needed change but didn't know how to go about it. I had been there for over 20 years, so walking away was not something that I could easily accomplish.

One day, my oldest daughter, Monea, who was 12 at the time, said to me, "Mom, I want to be saved, but not like this." Her statement really caused me to seek after God for guidance and direction. Blaine and I spoke about my feelings but didn't see eye to eye about me leaving the church. Frustrated with it all, I called several pastors and coincidentally, they all suggested that I visit Highway Word of Faith Church.

When God spoke to my spirit and gave me the go ahead, I was nervous and not sure if it really was God. My husband was not in agreement, but he did not stop me from weighing my options.

The kids and I went to Highway Word of Faith and after visiting several weeks, we wanted to become a part of the church family. My husband and I talked with the bishop and the first lady to explain our situation to them and asked them to cover me and my children while we were there. I made it clear that I did not want to officially "join" the church without my husband but that we would actively attend services.

That was the first time that our family was separated when worshipping God. Since the transition was a little hard for me, my husband and I started out going to each other's services at least once a month. He would come to Sunday school and the kids and I would go to his church. Little by little, that arrangement began to fade.

Eventually, Sunday mornings became too hard for me. I missed the connection my family had. We used to get up, greet each other, get dressed, get in the same car together, stop for breakfast, and head to church. I began to pray and ask God what His plan was because this could not be the end of our story. Nothing changed with us. However, I knew I could not go back to our old church and nothing would change my mind.

As time went on, I became more involved at Highway. Even though I was not an official member, I was a part of the pastoral committee, a Sunday school teacher, and the director of women's ministry. I faithfully served in that ministry for a little over five years until God began to take me in a new direction.

What was going on in my life was unexplainable. I felt like there was a war between my spirit and my feelings. I always desired to do the will of God, but there was a struggle of wanting to please others too.

When things are off in my life, I pray and ask God for His guidance. I cried out to God more and more regarding my family because I felt like we were drifting apart. The more I prayed, the more impossible it seemed for us to come back together again. I felt like our marriage was like crazy glue but with ministry, we couldn't get it to stick. The adhesive had worn off.

Sometimes Blaine would mention things that people would say like, "Are you and your wife still together?" and sometimes I would mention how I felt too, but after hearing each other out, we would wash our hands of the situation and keep things moving.

One night, I was sitting on my bed and I heard God say, "I'm about to bridge the gap." I didn't think much of it. The very next day, I was waiting for my clients to come to pick up their children and God said, "Get ready. I'm about to bridge the gap." I said to myself, "Okay, this must mean that God is about to have my family worship Him together again." I got happy like anyone who just received exciting news would because I believed that that's what God was telling me, and I prayed, asking for God to show me how. I knew that I wasn't going back to Blaine's church, and he wasn't coming to my church.

A few days later, God woke me up in the wee hours of the morning, so I went downstairs to pray. While I was in prayer, God gave me a glimpse of my husband and I, along with our two girls, in church praising Him. I was up preaching, and my husband was cheering me on. At that moment, I began to cry out of gratitude as I thanked God for showing me that vision. That morning, I shared the revelation with Monea, and she said, "Mom, I've been praying for the same thing!" It was comforting to know that we agreed.

As the day went on, I continued to thank God and out of nowhere, He said to me, "I'm calling you forward to bridge the gap." This time I asked, "Lord, what does that mean?" He said to me "You will pastor." I couldn't help but to laugh. When exactly was all of this meant to happen? I began to say the devil is a liar because pastoring was the furthest thing from my mind. Again, I heard God say that I would pastor, but I tuned that small voice out because I thought that I had been hearing things.

I heard the same thing for three days and I couldn't get away from it. I came up with what I believed was a good plan. I thought that if I told a few people about my vision, they would talk me out of believing it. Maybe they would laugh and say I was being silly or something. I started with a bishop who was around my age. Surely, he could confirm that I was tripping, but he didn't. He said, "Woman of God, it's about time." He had been praying for God to raise up pastors that he could plant in churches. I decided that he wasn't a good person to call since he thought somehow God was answering his prayer.

Next, I called my best friend, Gwann, and told her. I was certain she would tell me to stop playing, but she didn't. She prayed right on the spot, asking God to allow me to submit to His will and help me not to be afraid. Still not convinced, I talked to Monea, and she said, "Mom, I believe you can do it." Very confused, I tried to level with God. I figured I'd tell my husband and if he said no or had an uncertain response, I'd know it was not God speaking to me.

When it came time for me to tell Blaine what I believed God told me, I was scared. I recorded his response so others could hear him laugh at me, but he didn't. He said that if God is calling me, then do His will. I could not believe his response, and I *still* was not convinced. I was up for nights seeking God and praying. I was praying for more hours than I slept. About two weeks later, I was sitting at my computer and the spirit of God came over me and again I heard Him say, "You will pastor," and I jumped up and started screaming as if someone had died. I was praying telling God how I couldn't and why I shouldn't. I gave one excuse after another until I surrendered and said yes. Then it hit me; *this* was how God would bring me and my husband back together again, and I was sold.

When the time came for me to pastor, nothing changed. He came to the first service and left early to go to his church. I was crushed because I thought that this was God's way of molding us. Sunday after Sunday, he went his way, and I went mine. I started to feel a bit rejected, as if he was choosing something else over me. I told myself how silly that was, but it didn't make the feeling disappear.

I asked God for understanding. I really didn't want to pastor, but I thought I'd do it if it meant us being together again. Months went by, and Blaine continued to attend my service and leave in enough time to make his church service. Things weren't making any sense to me, but I had to trust God.

There's a song that became my anthem, "For Your Glory" by Tasha Cobbs. Every time I felt low, I would sing it over and over until it would resonate in my spirit. It didn't matter that I cried until my eyes swelled and that I couldn't breathe. I had to remind myself that God had a plan.

Pastoring without my spouse seemed like fishing without bait – pointless. *It's not about me*, I kept telling myself, but the more I said it, the less I believed it. The enemy would tell me, "What's the use?" People wouldn't understand how a God who is all-knowing and wise would call me into such a calling without my mate by my side. It constantly felt almost like someone punched me in gut and knocked the wind out of me.

While creating flyers for church events or a series, I would get mad because I could only put my picture on it, as if I wasn't married. I often felt like a single married woman and I hated that feeling. I just wished that by some miraculous change, my husband would wake up and see just how much I needed him.

It is my belief that God already spoke to Blaine and told him what to do, but he still plays both sides of the field. I think he is afraid to leap, and I also feel that he's punishing me so I can feel what he felt when I left his church. I don't know that any of that is even true, but I do know that too many people prophesied to me that my husband and I would do ministry together.

I have yet to come to grips with this part of my story, but I see that serving God and doing His will is an individual thing and obedience is better than sacrifice. For me, two things are certain – one, I don't want to live without Blaine, so I have to trust God in this area of my life and two, I have a longing desire to please the Lord. If Blaine never joins me in ministry, I will have move on.

What God is doing in my life is extraordinary and I can't be held back by the feelings of my heart. He has been blessing Transformation Worship Centre with sending in souls that are yearning for Him and just a little after a year of starting the ministry, God has blessed us with a church building. Though marriage is instituted by God, one cannot allow their feelings of it to supersede their ministry and walk with God.

Monique Bailey

My love for you grows day by day.
From moments of strength, to moments of weakness,
our love is solid in every way.
So, as we go through our ups and our downs
We find hope in our love that stands firm on solid
ground.

• *Patricia D. Harris*

In Sickness & In Health

3

In Sickness & In Health
Sandra Bailey

We made a vow to each other in the presence of God – I, Sandra /I, Roy take you to be my husband/wife, to have and to hold…for better, for worse, for richer, for poorer, *in sickness and in health…*

We've been there for each other through the years in the good times as well as the bad times, when our money was good and when our money was funny. We've weathered storms of sickness and enjoyed smooth sailing in health. However, one storm of sickness illuminates more than all the others we've endured. I remember that day in January of 2015.

It was a Friday morning. I was in my office at home working when my husband, whose name is LeRoy, but I affectionately call him Roy, came in and sat in the recliner. I normally worked in my PJ's and would shower later in the day, but this day I did something different; I got up, showered, got fully dressed as if I was going to the office aside from putting on my shoes. There was no reason for me to do this, but in retrospect, God was preparing us for the unknown.

We spoke to each other and I asked him how he was feeling. He began to express that his arm felt extremely heavy and he felt like a ton of bricks were resting on his chest. He also went on to tell me that he had similar feelings a couple of weeks or so before that morning. He was doing some renovations at his sister's home in Maryland and had a pain so sharp and intense that his knees buckled, and he fell into his truck. His sister witnessed it and wanted to call me, however, my husband convinced her it was nothing and not to call and worry me.

Let me tell you a little about my husband's character; he's what we call a "man's man". That is a man who takes pride in doing what he must do as a man for his family and always putting himself last. I know this more than ever after that memorable day in January.

While he was sharing how he felt, I sent an instant message to my supervisor stating I needed to log off due to a family emergency. I asked Roy if he wanted to go to the medical aid unit close to our house to avoid a long wait at the emergency room. He said yes but he wanted me to go with him, but he knew I was working. I said let's go, and that I had already taken care of work.

A couple of things resonated with me; one, he never seeks medical attention and two, because of the discomfort he was in, he wanted me to go with him. Thankfully, I was fully dress and only had to put on my shoes and a coat. I immediately called our youngest daughter, LaTrina, who was a registered nurse working at the University of Pennsylvania in the cardiac surgical unit. I informed her of what was going on and she said, "Take dad to the hospital." Since we had no idea what was happening, we opted for the medical aid unit for the sake of saving time.

We arrived at the medical aid unit, checked in and because of his symptoms, they took him in the back for examination quickly. They performed an EKG and said it was normal, however, the on-duty doctor was concerned about how Roy said he felt. Inevitably, we were instructed to go to the hospital just like Trina instructed us to do in the beginning. Once in the car, I called Trina back and told her where we were headed.

"Mom get dad to the hospital now; he is having a heart attack. I'm almost home because I left work at the first phone call. I will pick up Nana and meet you at the hospital."

We hung up our phones. My mind began to race in so many directions. *Heart attack?! What in the world? Is he going to be alright? What if I get him to the hospital and it's too late?* All these questions were running through my mind as I tried to remain as calm on the outside as possible. The last thing I wanted to do was add to the dilemma we were already in by alerting Roy to what was really happening to him.

In the meantime, Roy was asking me why I was driving so erratic and I tried dismissing his question by jokingly saying, "I'm trying to beat the rush of people that might be coming into the emergency room at the hospital since we have to go there now." Roy casually said to me, "You better slow this bad boy down before we don't get there at all." He chuckled a bit and he appeared to be okay. He didn't say he was in anymore pain nor did he show any outwards signs of distress such as shaking, sweating or anything of the sort.

We arrived at the Christiana Hospital Emergency Room rather quickly. I checked him in and told them we were referred to go there by the medical aid unit doctor. Of course, they didn't belabor getting him in the back. His vitals were checked and then on to the EKG. Roy was very thirsty, and the EKG technician told him he would get him some water as soon as the test was done, but that didn't happen because the technician took the EKG results so fast and left the room. The next thing we knew, Roy was being moved to an examination room with instructions to not drink anything.

Before they got him settled, a team of doctors, nurses, a phlebotomist and an ultrasound technician piled into the room and surrounded his bed. Soon enough, the doctors, nurses and phlebotomist all disappeared, leaving the ultrasound technician behind to continue his work. He still didn't find whatever he was looking for and finally said he would be back and try again but had an emergency in another room. Roy and I were alone for a while talking and laughing when suddenly the doctors and nurses rushed into his room and said, "Mr. Bailey, you are having a heart attack right now!" They needed to get him to the operating room immediately. While all of this was transpiring, I was struggling to process the abrupt diagnosis. Amidst the chaos, we were separated, which made me feel like we were being torn apart. Roy was being rushed into surgery and I was being ushered to the waiting room by a hospital employee telling me everything was going to be alright and that he would stay with me until family arrived.

I was so numb hearing Roy was having a heart attack. All I could think to do in that moment was call my pastor. When I got a hold of him, I told him what was going on and asked him to pray. See, we have two daughters and our oldest daughter, LaToya, a daddy's girl, was pregnant with her first child. I knew she needed to know what was happening to her dad, but I was so concerned for her health and the unborn baby. In all the panic, I called our son-in-law, Brandin, and told him what was going on. I needed him to pick up Toya from work so he could gently break the news to her. I called Roy's sisters and his uncle and aunt to make them aware of what was happening and just waited. Finally, Trina and my mother arrived followed by Toya and Brandin. Some family started to arrive, and many others called checking on him. The procedure seemed to take forever but after only about an hour and a half, the wait was over! The doctor came out and said Roy made it through the surgery and was going to be okay. We all were so grateful to God in that moment.

Once Roy got settled in his room, we were able to see him. He was eating his dinner and our daughters were checking things out and talking to him. About 10-15 minutes passed, and things were beginning to not feel right with me. I felt a tingling and numbness run down my left side. My face started to pull and tingle as well. I was very still and couldn't express what was going on to anyone in the room. I was sitting in the chair next to Roy's bed. The girls were talking to me and they said I wasn't responding correctly and began to slur my words. All the conversation seemed so far away from me and I wanted to ask everyone to speak up, but the conversation became even duller to the point where I couldn't focus on what was being said. I remember my husband's nurse, along with Trina and Toya, turning their full attention to me.

Roy's nurse and Trina's assessments were that I was possibly having a stroke. They rolled me from my husband's bedside to the emergency room. In the ER, the doctor came in to assess me and was talking so fast and suggesting a procedure to thin all my blood, which was very scary to me. I didn't understand, nor had I ever had that done. Trina assured me it was okay and at that moment I trusted what my daughter said and submitted to the procedure. The doctor explained that the procedure could only be safely done within 45 minutes of the initial symptoms, so once again, time and God proved to be on our side.

What a storm of sickness that was. Roy had a heart attack and I had a stroke the same day. This resulted in us being admitted into the same hospital, on the same day, on the same floor. That's just one example of how we really are one flesh and we carry each other in our spirit. Who would have thought that? Our family was visiting Roy in the Cardiac Intensive Care Unit then leaving to come visit me in the Neuro Intensive Care Unit. Roy was released to go home the next day and I had to remain in the hospital another day, so two days later, I was released to go home.

We also vowed for better, for worse, for richer, for poorer. It was the heart of winter and Roy couldn't work, but I was so thankful to God for sparing his life. Our daughters took charge. They didn't want us stressing, so they took over managing and budgeting our household expenses, making follow-up doctor appointments, getting our prescriptions filled and meal prepping. Anything we needed, they handled it! We couldn't ask for better daughters. We survived the sickness, but now we were hit with the worse - surviving while the storm passed over – Roy getting better and me staying well. It wasn't easy having the only significant income for three months. I could see the emotional stress weighing on Roy, as I told you in the beginning, he is a "man's man" and when he can't operate as such, other things start to creep in, like depression. During it all, I did what I knew to do and that is pray and I'm sure Roy, our daughters, my mom, and others were praying too.

Prayer is our weapon and the reason we've survived this long after all that we have been through. Because we made our vow to each other in the presence of God and have always incorporated prayer, even when we weren't doing everything right, God honored our consistency and kept us in the midst of the storm. We are still together – 35 years strong – maturing in age together, discussing our aches and pains but still thanking God for life, the activity of our limbs and a sound mind together, laughing together, crying together, enjoying our three grandchildren together, loving our daughters together, taking care of my mom together and looking out for one another. We are excited to see what our next chapter in life brings.

Stay true to your vows. It's not always easy, but it's doable with a lot of hard work, praying and keeping that third string in your marriage – God. Be blessed.

Sandra Bailey

When He chose me, I knew what I had to do,
There was no us, without including You!
Let's allow this relationship to evolve naturally and free from force,
To ensure our new family is set on the right course.
I am here for you as little or as much as you may need
Because when he chose me, I accepted you, as a part of me.

● *Patricia D. Harris*

Blended Families

4

Blended Families
Tanya Moorehead-Cooley, Ph.D.

"There will always be steps you can take toward unity in your blended family, and you will make it - one step at a time!" – Donna Houpe, *Becoming One Family*

Before I began my relationship with my husband, Travis, I never dreamt that I would be part of a blended family. I actually preferred to meet someone who did not have children. I wanted to begin parenthood together. I had a vision of the perfect family; I grew up in the *Cosby Show* generation, so that is what I wanted. I wanted to be the Huxtables, but after I met my husband, I began to see that being a stepmom, a "bonus-mom" as my husband affectionately called me, or whatever other clever names the mother who didn't give birth to the child but provides love to them is called, wasn't that bad of a role after all. I began to see that I was made for this. I had the love and the patience that was required in the job description.

To reassure myself that I was making the right decision, I made sure I asked a lot of questions while we were dating. It was important to me to know that my future husband had a good relationship with his children and their mother. I wanted to make sure that he loved and supported them. A lack of a healthy relationship would have been a deal breaker for me. So, I watched him, I fell in love with him, and then we all lived happily ever after. That sounds good, but that is not how our story ends. In fact, our story is not complete. Our story doesn't look anything like my vision of a blended family; in fact, it is almost the polar opposite.

It is important to note that I was raised in a successful, loving blended family. So why wouldn't I want a blended family if I knew the beauty of a blended family from my own life? I realized that the beauty that I experienced as a child wasn't always easy and it wasn't always beautiful. I recognized that it took work and sacrifice. I was not against the work, sacrifice, or the commitment necessary, but I figured if I could have a family that didn't have the extra layer of difficulty, why not select that one? It is hard for me to have a less than ideal blended family in my marriage with the knowledge that blended families have the potential to be amazing. There isn't a happily ever after in our story. Although I have given up several times, I still have hope because of my childhood story.

My Childhood Blended Family

My father had a daughter, my amazing sister, Leslie, before my parents met. My sister was raised by her mom and grandfather. She lived with them and her two siblings in the Midwest while we lived on the East Coast. To me, my blended family was beautiful. We had challenges like any family, and we did not see each other often. We had phone calls, letters, summer vacations, and occasional holiday visits. Why did I think that this was so beautiful? Well, my mother and my sister's mother gave us the opportunity to love each other and to know each other on top of giving us access to each other's respective families whom we were not connected to by blood. My sister's mom always introduced me to her family and friends as her daughter, and of course, my mother called my sister her daughter too.

As a child, I didn't understand the significance of a woman calling her ex's child her own. For my sister's mom to call me one of her daughters meant that she was open to loving me and subsequently let go of her pain or any negative emotions that she may have had due to her relationship with my father. I looked forward to my stepsons finding a special name for me. I eagerly looked forward to introducing my sons to my family and our amazing village and when I did, they welcomed them as I knew they would. I understand that my journey in accepting children that came before my relationship was much easier than the journey of the women who have to let go of specific emotions connected to a failed relationship that created lives.

How could I understand all of that as a child? I didn't understand that our mothers had to come to terms with accepting the fact that they were both intimate with the same man and had children with him. I wouldn't say that they were best friends, but I remember them being like sisters when we were all together. They shared laughs together and they shared my sister and me. My sister's mother died 17 years ago, but I believe she died knowing that my mother would step in and fill in the gap. That is exactly what she did and continues to do.

My family was not perfect, but I grew up with fond memories of family outings on the lake with my sister, her mother, and her siblings that I referred to as my sister and brother, our father, my mom and anyone else that was part of our extended families. I never knew that this wasn't a normal blended family experience until I was a young adult. I thought everyone in blended families had the same love and unity that we shared.

I loved my sister's family, especially her mom. I recall writing her a letter to thank her for the sacrifices that she and my mom made for us to have the relationship that we established when I was a child. I appreciate what my father contributed too, but even at an early age I understood that much of the power in making our blended family beautiful was in the hands of the women. So, with this example of excellence, I entered my own blended family. I entered it with great expectations. Although it didn't begin like we wanted it to, we were still open and ready for a beautiful, blended family.

Our Union

When my husband and I got married, my stepsons were not present. We saw them a month later and had a small, intimate ceremony that celebrated our family uniting. It was beautiful; we redid our vows and added vows for the boys to signify our commitment to them. We celebrated with a toast, dinner, and cake. The only thing that was missing was 100 guests and the reception hall. This took place in my childhood home with my parents, my sister-in-law, and my immediate family. The purpose was to show my new sons that they were important to us and our new family.

Shortly before we were engaged, tension between Travis and his ex grew and subsequently entered our lives, which made it challenging to build the foundation for a beautiful, blended family. When we began our relationship, my husband spoke to his children and their mother frequently. They did not have a formal custody arrangement through the courts, but he contributed financially and emotionally. This was their arrangement; it was not perfect, but it worked. Eventually, there were custody and child support orders issued by the court. I was in favor of this process. I felt more comfortable having a set plan in place to support the children. I had no idea that the process that I welcomed for our family would be accompanied by so much stress.

Something that I thought would help us move forward smoothly was more like playing an emotional adult version of tug-of-war. Everything felt like a fight, and we were constantly filled with anxiety because we never knew what was going to happen. My husband's ex was very reluctant to let the children visit us or allow us to talk to them on the phone. Things like seeing the children for the holidays felt like winning a battle but still having to keep watch for the enemy to attack when you least expected it. The analogy may sound a little extreme, but this was our reality. Even when the boys were with us, there was always this looming feeling that the good moments that we shared were going to be snatched away from us.

Unfortunately, our worst fears did come true. There was a period that we did not see and barely spoke to the boys for a little less than five years. Their mother later accepted the responsibility for the separation but at that point, the damage had been done. My family has and continues to overcome anger, confusion, pain and depression related to our broken blended family. It has had its ups and downs over the years, possibly more downs, but as the quote at the beginning of this chapter states, "There will always be steps you can take toward unity in your blended family, and you will make it - one step at a time!" I must admit that I don't always believe this, but the love that I have for my husband and my children, those that came before and after my marriage, drives me to never fully throw in the towel.

Distance

Like my beautiful, blended family experience growing up, my new blended family is separated by several states, which has added its fair share of challenges. We live in Connecticut and my stepsons live in Pennsylvania. The boys lived with their mom and we briefly shared some holidays and summer vacations with them. We would have been able to spend more time together if we didn't live so far away from each other.

Blended families can work with distance - I know because I was part of one, but if you can decrease the distance in miles between you and the children, do it. This was not the case for us, although, in the spirit of making our blended family work, we did extend the invitation to my husband's ex to move to our state because we have an amazing family and a supportive village that would have welcomed her and her sons.

My husband's ex is a single mom. I wanted to share the parenting load with her. I knew that it would not be easy, but I offered it to her. We both offered it to her. She did consider it and the benefits of living closer but decided not to move. In a perfect world, she and the boys would live a few miles away from us and we would occasionally have family dinners together and the boys would have access to all of us whenever they needed us.

The Future

My beautiful, blended family story wasn't always beautiful, but I don't have any memories of the tough parts because my parents and my sister's mother never stopped working together. The good truly overshadows the tough times. My father said he always had a dream of having my sister nearby even though she lived in the Midwest and we were on the East Coast. He never stopped dreaming and believing that it would happen. Currently, my sister and her family, my family, and my parents all live within three miles of each other. Even though it's tough, I will keep believing and dreaming of a beautiful, blended family for my household.

Our oldest sons are 17 and 18, and we have two sons that live with us that are two and five years old. I dream of a day when we will all be together for the holidays, school graduations, weddings, birthdays, and even regular days. I will never stop believing that we can heal from the pain of the past and begin something new that will overshadow the obstacles and pitfalls that we had to overcome to get to a brighter future together. I wish that I could conclude this chapter with a "we all lived happily ever after." Our blended family isn't beautiful yet, but we are working on it. Family is always worth the fight.

Things to consider as you prepare for a blended family:
1. Do you want to be part of a blended family? Be honest with yourself first and then with your potential mate. Talk to others in blended families. Every story is unique, but each one has valuable lessons that will help you as you make the decision about entering a blended family.
2. What are your expectations? It is a good idea to identify them before you go into the marriage or at least establish them early in the marriage so you can work towards them together. Like number one, talking to other families will help you identify some elements that you aspire to have in your blended family. I caution you to not get discouraged when it doesn't look exactly like you want it to. It is still good to have a vision of what you want your family to look like, what you want your family to do together and how you want to support each other.
3. Are the key adults willing to work together on behalf of the children? This might be the most important thing to consider. If the adults work together and put their differences aside, the potential is limitless.

Working together solves issues of custody, child support, visits, shared holidays, discipline, and support on every level. Our biggest challenge is the lack of unity with the adults in our blended family. Even though we are not blended the way I envisioned us to be, we are still a blended family. I believe that we could have made tremendous progress over the years if we were able to work together and move beyond our differences.

4. Are you ready to work through the tough parts to get the beauty? Well, I am still asking myself this question. Our two oldest sons are young men now and we are still working through the tough parts. My husband and I have thrown in the towel momentarily but the blessing is that we have rarely done it at the same time. We support each other through it. I recognize when my husband needs to step back and he does the same thing for me. We also have trusted friends that help us to process the tough parts so we can make wise decisions.

5. Are you willing to see a therapist? We have welcomed the support of a licensed family therapist. Blended families come with baggage that needs to be sorted out. Even if the relationships appear to be going well, it never hurts to have an occasional check in with a

therapist, so all voices are heard in a supportive environment. Even if you are not able to visit the therapist together, it is important to gain the support of a professional if necessary. I have experienced a myriad of emotions throughout this process – love, excitement, hurt, confusion, frustration and an overall sense of bewilderment. I am glad that I gave myself and my family the opportunity to receive the support from a therapist.

6. Love covers a multitude of sins. Are you willing to show love even when it isn't given to you? I said number three was the most important, but I may have changed my mind. Love, unconditional love, is at the top of the list. Love for yourself and every member of your blended family and that includes the spouse's ex too. I have tried my best to continue to demonstrate acts of love even when it was hard. This journey with my blended family has taught me patience and how to love at all times. I haven't mastered it, but I am committed to working on it.

Tanya Cooley, Ph.D.

I think of the day, the sleepless nights
and I wonder if these thoughts becoming reality, are in sight.
I know you already, I can feel your touch, I can hear your cry,
And I wonder if it will never become a reality,
No matter how hard we try

● *Patricia D. Harris*

Marriage & Infertility

5

Marriage & Infertility
Kiara Moore, LPCMH

My name is Kiara Moore, MA, LPCMH. I'm a licensed professional counselor working with children, adults, couples and families. On May 21, 2011 I married my husband, Pedro Moore.

Pedro and I were introduced and essentially hooked up by our pastor. We went to the same church but in different locations. Our pastor came up with a lame excuse insisting we needed to meet and exchange contact information to work on some project. There was no project, but we had an instant connection and knew early on that we were meant to be. Breaking all my rules, the first date lead into an unofficial, yet official relationship. Not wasting any time, we were engaged within six months and married one year from our proposal.

When I pictured my life and my family, I always imagined having a fun and happy marriage with about three children. I wanted a thriving career, so I knew that having children would have to wait awhile, especially since I was married at 23 years old. I spend most of my time with children and seem to have a great way of connecting with them, so being the best mom was a title I knew I could live up to.

In 2013, I finished graduate school, we bought a house, and seemed to hit many of our marriage goals, so we had the talk and decided we were ready to start our family. It was an unusually warm day in December, so we went for a walk and planned out what we assumed would be the next few months of our lives. I knew many couples who experienced infertility and many more couples who overcame infertility, but I never imagined that we too would have this experience.

As impulsive as I am, I become impatient very early on.

Why isn't this happening?

What's going on?

Is something wrong with me?

I waited. I did everything right so why am I not pregnant yet?

That year was a hard year. We stood by, wanting and hoping, while at least 13 friends, family members, and acquaintances announced their pregnancies. Yes, you read that right – 13. I am not a jealous person and was genuinely happy for each of them, but I was also eager, hurt, and starting to get angry. Little did I know, this was just the beginning of the wait. Most doctors won't see you until you've tried for at least a year. We waited, prayed and suffered as a couple silently while people asked us those painful questions such as, "When are y'all going to start having some babies?" or "Don't y'all want kids?" I answered the questions playfully in the beginning but later began to dread certain social obligations because I knew the questions were coming at least once or twice. Once the doctors' visits began, I was even more concerned because everything was coming back fine. It wasn't until about three years into our journey that we received the most devastating news.

Our doctor told us that we could not conceive naturally and that our only hope was in vitro fertilization, also known as IVF. IVF is when the sperm and egg are both extracted, fertilized, and later implanted in the uterus. This series of procedures cost on average, $15,000-20,000. We were devastated, crushed, and grieved. At that moment, I quickly denounced the doctor's words and told her that I was not accepting her report. This is when my curiosity in our anatomical makeup and hope in the doctors ended and my faith in God activated into turbo gear. I wrestled with the idea but later declared that my only hope was in God and that He was going to perform a miracle, or we just would not have kids of our own.

After four years of suffering infertility issues, I found out I was pregnant! No IVF, just faith put into action. On May 21, 2017, I gave my husband the best anniversary gift ever, the news that he was officially getting a new title – Daddy.

While experiencing infertility for over four years, we faced many challenges and there were moments when our marriage suffered. Challenges have a way of building stronger people or breaking people down. Infertility, though not discussed often, is much more common than most people think. If you find yourself facing infertility, know that you are not alone. You are not the problem, and it isn't anyone's fault! Here are a few tips to help you through your journey.

1. You are not in this alone.

Although infertility was a challenge we faced together within our marriage, it was also a battle we fought alone. There were times when we were feeling down at the same time and times when we had to lift each other up. There were also times when I didn't want to trigger my husband if he seemed as if he was having a good day, so I held in my pain and isolated my feelings. There were times I felt alone and that he didn't understand, and vice versa. When I remembered that we were in this together, I could be comforted. It is my job to be there for others and there are so many times that I need others to be present for me but letting people in is also hard for me to do. I had to open up, be vulnerable, and allow myself to let out what was suffocating me inside.

2. Your spouse is not the enemy.

It is easy to forget why you're upset when you feel upset all the time. As if the cloud of infertility wasn't hard enough to bare, I tragically lost my only brother. I fell deep into my grief and was overcome by the nature of his death and the challenges my entire family now faced. I was grieved, angry and extremely anxious. I continued to work because helping others with their problems kept me from having to face my own. I was spiraling. I became a person that I didn't recognize and one I didn't even like. I was not a good wife either. I was short-tempered and just mean. I couldn't always control it. I had to apologize often, and I had to try very hard to reel myself back in. Thankfully, I have a very patient husband who loves me and understood me, even when I didn't understand myself. I had to remind myself at times that although I was mad at the world and at times God, my husband was not my enemy. It is hard to overcome infertility if you are constantly at odds. God is a miracle worker but unless your name is Mary, there's a certain part you both must play in order for your miracle to manifest.

3. Don't overthink it.

This challenge that we faced was not the result of any mistakes or bad choices. It was biology and ultimately God's timing, which we had no control over. I knew my body so well, too well, that I could literally feel when I was ovulating. I had fertility monitors and calendar reminders. I bought dollar store pregnancy tests by the handfuls since buying multiple name brand tests became very expensive. Naturally, having the "it's biology" mindset got old quick; it overcomplicated things and just took the fun out of the sex. So, one day, I decided to stop. Stop overthinking, stop testing, stop tracking. Let's just have fun and get back to enjoying each other. This was when we began to reconnect.

4. Talk it out.

We were blessed that our infertility journey ended, but I know that this isn't always the case. Talk about your options. Have a plan B, C and D. Discuss your limitations and be honest. Don't suffer in silence. Infertility can have dark and devastating effects. Go to individual and couples counseling or support groups. You are not alone.

The best advice I can give couples who are facing any challenge is to remember why you fell in love. Remember why you chose him/her. Remember why you married each other. You should never try to get back to a time when life was better or focus on what was. We don't usually consider how different life was during those "good times" and the difference in responsibilities. The best we can do is focus on the here and now. Ask yourself these questions: *What can we do at this moment during this challenge? Do we need to reconnect?* Take off the boxing gloves and end the war. Take a vacation and release the stresses of life. Whatever the case, focus on right now. You may not have what you want, be where you want to be, or have the family you've dreamed of when you were 10 years old, but you do have each other. When you face your challenges together, side by side, you will win *every time*.

Kiara Moore, LPCMH

I acknowledge who you are, I see you.
From the glow of your skin, to the brownness of your eyes, I see you.
The way you glide when you walk, to the soft sounds of your voice when you talk,
I acknowledge who you are, I see you.
I see you; I see you with my heart

● *Patricia D. Harris*

Interracial Marriage

6

Interracial Marriage
Candice Resto

"Yoke" Status

My perception of being "equally yoked" was that my "future husband" had to come from the same background, share the same religious beliefs, and have the same education level along with a whole laundry list of false beliefs.

What I later studied was that in the Christian faith, to be "equally yoked" simply means when two people are believers in God. If a mutual spiritual connection is shared, I believe God can allow both believers to be on one accord and fulfill his plan through each other's lives. Like in everything, having a routine check-up is always good practice, so I always try to do a periodic "yoke status", sort of like a check-up or check-in, if you will.

"Single" Status

Pulse Check: When I first met my husband, William, I had already dealt my fair share of lackluster relationships, and let's just say, I was not looking for a soulmate at that time in my life. Little did I know, God was already making plans for our paths to meet at his appointed time.

God used a mutual relationship, who happens to be my now sister-in-law, to bring him and I together. One day, Aida had her vivacious and persistent brother call into our workplace to let us know that she would be running a little behind schedule. His deep, baritone voice sparked some curiosity. We met and soon became friends. I helped him write his first essay for a college paper and library dates turned into dinner dates, which then turned into us having family gatherings together.

This was my first interracial relationship so up until that point, I had never experienced so many prejudices or learned how to deal with them. To make matters worse, we both received some negative feedback from both sides of our families. The last place I expected ridicule to come from was from our own flesh and blood, but I realized that people are very afraid of what they don't understand. We heard comments like, "Don't go mixing our blood up with those people" and "Our family don't believe in mixin' races". We were okay as long as we kept our relationship in the friend zone. Both sides of our family made it known that if our relationship went any further, we would never hear the end of it.

During our courtship, I recall going on a date with Will to the Baltimore Harbor. We planned a day at the harbor followed by dinner at the famous Phillips Seafood restaurant. As we began leaving the restaurant, we noticed people staring and talking openly and loudly. We assumed there was a celebrity nearby stirring up all the commotion. William overheard a group of people talking about us and stood up to them for the both of us. It turned out that they were members of a Greek frat visiting Phillips Restaurant and some of them were seemingly upset that we were together. The situation became so intense that we had to quickly leave the harbor.

That was our first meeting with intolerance as a couple and it was only the beginning. As years continued to pass, we continued to deal with the same pushback from all sorts of people. The strange part is that in 1995, we were still experiencing racism as if we were back in 1965, but God already had a specific plan for both of our lives, so he ensured that we were equipped and prepared to deal with every situation that we would face. In the book of Isaiah, we are reminded:

"No weapon that is formed against thee shall prosper; and every tongue that shall rise against thee in judgment thou shalt condemn." (Isaiah 54:17)

"Engaged" Status

Pulse Check: At the tender age of 23, becoming engaged never crossed my mind. However, it didn't take Will long to pop the question. Growing up I never spoke to my mother, aunts or any other adult family member about marriage so I had very little guidance about what it meant to be a good and suitable helpmeet to my future husband. One day, a good friend asked me if I wrote in a journal. At that time, I didn't know what journaling was, but once she explained it to me, I was on my way to a life changing experience. I asked God to show me how to be the best possible helpmeet to my future husband and for our spirits to continue to be on one accord.

I wrote down every aspect of our relationship; I would journal about where we currently were at spiritually and where God wanted to take both of us spiritually. I also journaled about the church we should attend together as well as our commitment and covenant to each other and most importantly, to God. I spoke to God about our days being engaged and leading up to our wedding day along with the days to follow. Journaling became a daily habit, and as my faith continued to grow, my journaling became a sacred time that I enjoyed spending with God. This appointed time became so important to me because it was my time to listen and gain instruction along with Godly wisdom. I was able to communicate and express my gratitude, my inner thoughts and my prayer request to God.

Journaling taught me patience and reassurance that God was and still in complete control of every aspect of our lives. I would hear God's still voice say, "*Be still and know that I am God,*" (Psalm 46:10). Putting my trust completely in God and leaning on his word allowed me to rest in assurance that "*all things work together for our good for those who love the God, to those who are the called according to His purpose,*" (Romans 8:28).

In the beginning of our courtship back in 1994, Will did not attend church with me. I was once asked to speak at a church, and I invited him to attend with me. When we pulled up to the church, he decided he was not going to go inside with me. I was completely devasted and shocked, but I had to go ahead without him. Instead, he told me that he was going over to his relative's house who lived close by and would be back to pick me up. I couldn't believe he changed his mind at the very last minute. I said to myself, "This jive turkey, the nerve of him". When he arrived to pick me up, he asked me how it went, and I told him I was a bit nervous but made it through. Surprisingly, I wasn't upset, and we didn't discuss the situation any further because I understood this was something he was not comfortable with doing.

Fast forward, one day as I was getting ready for Sunday service and I noticed that he was to getting ready for church too. I didn't know if this was his way of making up from the last situation but without being pressured or being nagged, he joined me from that day forward. In my journal, I asked God to allow a Catholic man and a Pentecostal woman to be able to share both of our beliefs together. I was not ready to convert to a religion that I knew very little about and miss my father preaching every Sunday while I sit behind the pulpit. William was also not ready to leave a religion he grew up in as an altar boy for years and was accustomed to. God allowed us to find a non-denominational place of worship where we could learn about God and still retain our individual beliefs. I am sure it was the Holy Spirit and the gift of learning how to journal that my dear friend shared that helped to lead my king into God's ultimate plan and promise for his life and mine. I soon started to see our petitions made before God come to pass.

"Married Status"

Yoke Check-up: Twenty-four wonderful years later with two amazing children, I often wonder where the time goes. I would not have wanted to take this amazing journey with anyone else at my side. My chosen one, the head of my household, devoted and loving husband and my best friend and I have shared so many wonderful memories that will last us a lifetime and beyond. We were both re-baptized together at our home church, Faith City Family Church, and there we serve together and learn about God's word. Having a strong Christian household that instills God's teaching and seeks his daily guidance has allowed each one of us to personally experience God's amazing works that are manifested daily in our lives.

Our union along with the unconditional love of God has truly been nothing short of phenomenal. I am truly thankful and grateful to God for all his blessings both seen and unseen!

"Love is patient, love is kind. It does not envy, it does not boast, it is not proud. It is not rude, it is not self-seeking, it is not easily angered, it keeps no record of wrongs. Love does not delight in evil but rejoices with the truth." (1 Corinthians 13:1)

In life, we will all experience good times and some bad times, but just as Matthew 11:30 says, when God chooses who he desires each one of us to share those experiences with, "he makes the yoke easy and the burden light."

Candice Resto

There was a time your dreams were contained within four steel walls,
But by God's grace and mercy, He allowed those walls to fall.
Through it all you were not afraid to dream again,
And I am blessed to take this walk with you to the end!

● *Patricia D. Harris*

Supporting Your Spouse's Dreams

7

Supporting Your Spouse's Dreams
Christina Watlington, Ph.D.

I am 45 at the time I am writing this, and I have been married to my best friend for 25 years. On September 7, 2019, we celebrated our Silver Anniversary. During the ceremony, we were blessed to have our two children, Ngozi, our 24-year-old daughter, and Sadiki, our 19-year-old son, share our love story through their original poem. Their poem brought tears to our eyes because they eloquently captured the unfolding of our love over the years because, after all, they witnessed it.

I couldn't have imagined, when I was a young college student pregnant with Ngozi, where I would be today - married to an amazing man with the most amazing children ever. I couldn't have imagined as a young woman that two young people could turn every challenge into opportunities and beat the odds every step of the way, but what I didn't know then, I hold as a scripture to my soul now. There's power in having a strong tribe. There's power in having a spouse who has your back. The power that resides in that kind of love can give you faith and courage to move through life with confidence, determination, grace, and poise.

So, our love story, which is my favorite love story, is not one made from straight lines and perfect plans. Rather, it's a love story that has crooked lines, wonderful detours, and struggle. The messiness of our love is what I find to be the most beautiful. So, as I retell our story in this chapter, I will also share a few lessons I learned along the way.

In the Beginning: Pre-Marriage

At 18, I was a shy, young sister who was just beginning the next chapter of my life at college. I had many big dreams because I am dreamy like that. In fact, if left with enough time on my hands, I can get lost in a beautiful myriad of dreams. I love dreaming and I love planning.

As a college student at a conservative, small private college called Franklin & Marshall (F & M), I initially dreamed of becoming a lawyer. F & M was a school known for preparing students who are interested in attending law school. I knew I was on the right path and I had two scholarships to help me keep my eyes on the prize. F & M was out in the middle of nowhere in Lancaster, Pennsylvania so I wasn't concerned about having any huge distractions. I was in the right environment – boring, remote, and only a handful of brothers on campus – to keep me focused. Well, so I thought. Life has a way of challenging your assumptions. Mine were challenged when I saw a beautiful distraction that would change the trajectory of my life in the most extraordinary ways.

The first week of college was freshmen orientation week, and I was walking across the quad when I saw the beautiful distraction. This beautiful distraction's name was Damian, who would later change his name to Malik, and he was *fine*. My heart skipped a beat at the very sight of his fineness. Damian was wearing a Malcolm X pendant, advertising to others that he had a good dose of consciousness in him. Fine and intelligent were a good combination, so I was even more enamored by him. I wanted to get to know this guy, and it turned out that he wanted to get to know me too. We talked a few times during our freshmen year, but it wasn't until sophomore year that we began dating and by the summer before our junior year, I was pregnant.

I said our love was messy, right? This wasn't a planned pregnancy. The recipe for this unplanned pregnancy was living in a house together, listening to too much R & B (unfortunately that included some R. Kelly hits) and deciding that the pull-out method would be our birth control plan. We were smart, but we put intelligence on the shelf that summer, and because of that, we were going to have a baby.

I was scared and nervous. I remember crying myself to sleep that night after I learned I was pregnant. I had a conversation with my daughter who was growing inside me and I knew it would be okay. *We* would be okay. A few days later, Damian proposed to me and we were married on August 27, 1994, only days before we would start our junior year of college. That summer, I learned the importance of being guided by faith and courage, even when you're scared, and they have been important companions in my life ever since that time.

Early Marriage

Post-marriage, we moved off campus, found a nice lady, Carmen, to watch Ngozi when we were both in school, and Malik picked up a job (3rd shift) at a candy factory. He always smelled sweet like licorice those days. Malik and I graduated from college on time, in May of 1996. Our daughter, Ngozi, walked across the stage with us: one in the first of many proud moments we've shared over the years.

After graduation, we moved to Philadelphia and began our professional life. I worked as a research assistant at Hahnemann University at the Center for the Treatment & Study of Anxiety, because I planned on getting my doctorate in clinical psychology. Malik began his career in education as a teacher.

By 1998, I was ready to apply to doctoral programs and Malik was very supportive. I remember telling him that maybe I should apply to master's programs instead. Doctoral programs are highly competitive and very rigorous. As a young woman with a child, I thought I should be more realistic. Even though faith and courage were my new friends, sometimes they would abandon me.

As my number one supporter, he gave me sage advice. He encouraged me to apply to doctoral programs and see how that worked out for me. *"If it didn't work out, we could consider a master's program."* Notice that Malik said "we". Malik has always been good at focusing on our individual pursuits as collective pursuits. His collectivist approach to our marriage has been a critical ingredient in the success of our marriage. Whenever I doubted myself over the years, Malik has served as the angel on one shoulder who spoke louder than the devil on the other shoulder. He always has my back and guess what? I got accepted into every doctoral program that I applied to. I was on my way to becoming a clinical psychologist, and Malik was cool with us packing our bags and moving to Baltimore, Maryland.

Once we arrived in Baltimore, life gave us another surprise. I was pregnant again, this time with a boy, and I was about to start a very rigorous program. I wasn't as scared this time because I was gradually becoming better at breathing in courage and faith, while exhaling anxiety. When I didn't breathe in courage and faith, Malik would offer me the oxygen mask to do so and it all worked out. In 2005, I graduated from the University of Maryland, Baltimore County with my Ph.D. in Clinical Psychology. Ngozi was 10 at the time and Sadiki was five.

Over a Decade Married: Marriage Challenges

Malik and I renewed our vows for the first time, after being married for 10 years. We were making gains in our life and feeling good about life as it was and where it was heading. Malik went back to earn his Master's in Education. I began working as a psychologist at the VA Hospital. We eventually moved to Delaware so Malik could manage one of his first big leadership opportunities at a Career School outside of Philadelphia, while I managed a leadership opportunity at the Veterans Affairs Maryland Healthcare System.

During this period, we faced marital challenges. Malik was working long hours, and I was feeling exhausted from the long commute to work and running a new program for returning veterans. About 12 years into our marriage, we were losing our rhythm and our emotional connection to each other. It was during this time, that we began seeing a marriage counselor who could help us get back on track. We needed to sharpen our communication skills; we needed to pay attention to each other's emotional needs, and we needed to remember the art of compromise and processing grievances so they don't linger.

That was a pivotal time in our marriage because it was a reminder that marriage is something that you must consciously attend to just like other areas of your life. Marriage it not about the love you had at the beginning but about the journey you share with your partner as you continue building the love all the way to the end.

As a result of this experience, we now have several books on marriage that are part of our library. We use them as a guide when we need a tune-up. We will even schedule an evening each week to have marriage conversations. We have not been married for 25 years because marriage is a stroll in the park. We've been married for that long because we plan on building our love all the way to the end, and we lean on the right resources to help us do just that.

Starting Our Own Businesses

In December 2014, Malik successfully defended his dissertation and earned his Doctorate in Educational Leadership from the University of Delaware. There were now two doctors in the house. We both had been working together in high-level positions at a large human services organization and we both questioned if we were really living our passion in our respective roles.

I had been running a private practice part-time, where I was seeing a handful of clients each week. Malik was becoming more interested in restorative practices and he was already dazzling people with his trainings on this topic.

By October 2017, I grabbed hold of my good companions, faith and courage, and resigned from the company where we had been working. Malik, once again, was my biggest supporter. Later in 2018, Malik resigned from the same company to give attention to his company, Akoben, which was rapidly growing. In 2018, we did something very bold. We both walked away from working for others so we could give more attention to helping people through our own businesses. Interestingly enough, my psychology office is located right next door to his professional training office, Akoben. Even in business we are side by side.

Lessons Learned:

As I said in the beginning, our love story has crooked lines, wonderful detours and struggle. Malik and I were young when we started this amazing journey together. I was raised by my mother and my parents divorced when I was five. The idea of marriage didn't make me jump for joy when I was young. Malik's biological father died before he was even born, and his mother died right after our daughter was born. We didn't come from "perfect" homes (whatever perfect is) but we knew a little something about love and fighting for love. We also figured things out along the way.

When we had our children, we gave each of them an African naming ceremony. Ngozi's name means blessing. Sadiki's name means faithful and trustworthy. Our children have names that are meaningful and aligned with important values that set the tone for how they will live their lives. Malik and I have the following values that set the tone for our marriage:

1. Hold each other up
2. Be the number one cheerleader for your spouse
3. Focus on what's strong, not what's wrong
4. Don't take each other for granted
5. Spend valuable time with family
6. Tap into your gifts and talents even if it's scary to do so
7. Live a life of service
8. Give each other the benefit of the doubt

In the messiness of our love, we leaned into each other and held each other up. We formed beautiful bonds with our children. We have done things that seem impossible but were possible because we believed in each other and knew our collective potential.

Christina Watlington, Ph.D.

I don't want to count the minute nor the hour, the day, week, month or year.
I want to experience the wholeness of your mind, the gentleness of you touch and your warm embrace every minute, hour, day, week, month and year, you are near.

● *Patricia D. Harris*

Marriage & Longevity

8

Marriage & Longevity
Mary Ernestine Chance, MDiv

Statistic: According to the National Center for Family and Marriage Research at Bowling Green State University, only about 17 percent of married adults have been married for at least 40 years. Staying married for a lifetime is tough.

Deacon Melvin Chance and his wife Reverend Mary Ernestine Chance share the ups and downs of a marriage and factors that have allowed them to stay successfully married for 58 years.

We have been married 58 years. We have four daughters, four grandchildren, three great-grandchildren, and a host of spiritual daughters, sons and grandchildren.

What are the most memorable moments within your Marriage?

Ernestine: All I know is that my prayer was answered through my loss of my first husband, our joining together and Melvin being everything that a husband could be. To show me the love and respect for all my children, I could never love him enough for that. He always helped me with the children in every way that he could. One memorable example is during the time we were living in Brooklyn, New York. When I went to graduate school, he took on much of the housework, which I was glad I didn't have to do. It allowed me to focus on studying. He adjusted his work schedule so that when I had to go to school during the day, he was there with the children and he took good care of them. He would pick me up and when I came home, everything was decent and in order. There were rarely complaints about anything.

We had a great love for each other. And it has gone on from the beginning and it's still alive today. He never leaves this house, nor do we don't depart from each other without expressing love. We don't just say it. We try to do it and show the love of Jesus wherever we go. I know it's because we love the Lord and we give Him all the praise for keeping us in a joyous, peaceful relationship.

Talk about a challenging time and how you got through it.

Ernestine: Whatever he went through, the struggles and difficult times, I went through it along with him. As far as challenges, in the past few years we have both suffered health issues. We're in our eighties. It makes our life together even more precious. You can always make more money. But you can't always make more memories. So, with God, and help from our children, immediate family and church family, together we both intend to make the rest of our life, the best of our life.

Your children say their father still opens the car door for you. How does that make you feel, and does he ever get teased about it from others?

Ernestine: I feel very good about it. Why shouldn't I? From the first time we met, he would always open the door for me, and I took advantage of it. That was before we got married. It continues today. After we got married, he couldn't stop. I had a brother Joseph. He has passed on, but Joseph would always tease Melvin in front of me, saying, "Look at him, look at him; always opening the door for you." I teased him back, saying, "Your wife would be happy if you opened the door for her." Honestly, it's not a show.

It's no put on. Melvin always does it, even if the car is in the garage. When nobody's around, he opens the door. I feel good about all the loving gestures he does for me. People do tease him about why he's always doing that. But I tell my pastor and everyone, you need to open the door for your wife. My pastor teasingly says, "I'm not doing all of that!" My husband treats me like I'm his queen. He never stopped from day one.

What role does God play in your marriage?
Ernestine: We seek Him first, no matter what. If there is a disagreement, we come to grips with it. We don't stay mad or let the sun go down on our wrath. We just continue to ask God to give us a kinder spirit. Give us love for each other. And no matter what it is, we come to an agreement, even if it's agreeing to disagree about something. That has always been our way of life. Putting God first and seeking him. We certainly do it more now that we have gotten up in age. I can truly say if you put your trust in God, He will help you through any circumstance. There is nothing, no problem too hard for God.

What do you love about your spouse?
Ernestine: My husband met me during a difficult time in my life. I had lost my first husband, and I had two children both

under the age of two. He met me. We dated and fell in love and we got married. God gave me what I asked for. A loving, devoted husband. Someone who would love me and be good to my children. And as far as I know, what I have seen in my husband is that he was always a loving father. Even though I had two children when he married me, I can truly say he never made a distinction between any of our daughters in my presence. He took on my two children. We had two children together, and we raised our four daughters together. He was always there. He is a man that has always looked out for me and stood with me, through thick and thin. I'll always cherish him because of the peace and joy that we have in our marriage. I love him dearly and I always will.

What is a typical day like for you that shows your love for each other?

Ernestine: Once we're up and about, I like to go out and visit the sick. I visit my sister at the nursing home. My husband and I also see other residents and give them a word of comfort from the Lord, encouraging them and letting them know how much Jesus cares. When I'm home, my ministry includes calling those who are sick and shut in. I like to call my children every day and see how they're doing. Most of all, Melvin and I spend time together, watching tv, mostly

Christian programming. We have a good day together. No matter what the situation is, we just love each other and are there for each other. We don't know what it is to go anyplace too long without the other. We love spending time together in the Lord.

How important is communication in a marriage?

Ernestine: My husband and I share. We have to let each other know when we don't feel well with whatever is on our mind or whatever we are going through. We have to communicate and talk to each other about it. If it's something that you need or want, you share it. If you don't communicate it will put distance in your marriage. It's not just being there in the house or being together. You've got to know each other's mind and heart and talk with them and know what is really going on and show respect and love for each other. I don't know if my husband could show any more love for me than he already does. And I try to do the same for him and be there for him in every way. If a marriage is to grow, if a marriage is to be filled with love, don't let communication drop by the wayside. You must talk to let each other to know what's on your heart and mind. It's important to listen to each other and ask, "How is your day going?" or, "What would you like to do? Communicate and it will help to keep the marriage alive. We communicate and show our love and respect for each other, not just when we get out in public; we show it to each other right here at home, show love every day of our lives. The communication should first start with God. We talk to Him, even before we pray together, and we pray together every day. However, we first talk to God. At the end of the day we still talk to God. By doing that, your love is going to spread. Not just in your life, but you'll see it around you. Your actions will touch someone else's life when they see what God is doing in your life. Communicate with each other and you'll be a blessing to each other. Share love with each other every day.

What are some activities that you enjoy doing together?
Ernestine: It's always good to be with family. I include my husband's siblings with my brother and sisters. We try to come together. I love to cook meals during the holidays as I do on a regular basis. We spend time sharing fond memories, but the best part of my life is sharing with my husband. I love when we travel to New York and Mississippi to see our daughters, sons-in-law and the grands. We have extended family with our daughters' blended families. We also have members in the church who have adopted us as their mom, dad and their grandparents. We thank God for giving us that kind of love and we extend our love. However, there are some broken relationships in my

family. I'm praying that God will bring them all together to become loving because God blessed us so, and we have such a happy, joyous, peaceful marriage. I don't want to see broken relationships with my cousins, nieces and nephews. Our prayer is for God to bring them together in love while they have the chance. Tomorrow may be too late because Jesus may come at any time. But if I can in some small way encourage my relatives to get their lives in order and show love for other family members, then I feel my living will not be in vain. I reach out and show love to the family as much as I can through phone calls, cards and letters, and fellowship. Thanks to my husband and children, I even send messages to them on Facebook.

Your Husband has stood by you when you have had to take care of family members.

Ernestine: Any time I have had to be a caregiver, my husband has always stood by my side and been right there for my parents, sisters and brothers. He's been amazing and I thank God for him.

Talk more about your Bereavement Ministry to Funerals and Hospitals:

Ernestine: We reach out to members who are in our church family. We may reach out to others because of a church member that's connected. We don't have to know the person. My husband and I try to go together to comfort them and show them love in their time of grief. We go to the funeral. If we hear of someone's death, we don't always wait until the funeral. We will go by the house to see the family and offer words of encouragement. We love doing it, working for the Lord.

What message would you share with couples who aspire to have longevity in marriage?

Ernestine: Pray and ask God to lead and direct your path. I recommend Proverbs 3:5 and 6: "*Trust in the Lord with all of thine heart. Lean not to thine own understanding. In all thy ways acknowledge Him and He will direct your path.*" You may have some understanding, however my advice to you is to put God first, and then make sure you keep your spouse first. After God, they come first. Seek God, trust him, let Him lead you, and let Him direct your path. If you have other things in mind and you don't put God first, everything will not be in place, but if you put Him first, I believe you will have a happier union.

I'm a witness of what God can do in a marriage when you seek Him and put Him first. My advice for any couple is to show love, be there for each other. Let your husband know you love him. Let your wife know you love her. Do things together. Keep each other happy. We enjoy our church life together. And seeking God first will help in any union.

We continue to share our lives together by the grace of God. We thank God for our loving daughters and their husbands, for our grands and great grands, family and friends. I pray that God will continue to bless my children, that they will have a happy marriage like God has blessed us with for over 58 years. That's our prayer. On our knees, we lift them up in prayer every day. God is a great God and He will bring many things to pass.

We thank God for the cherished years of our lives together. The moments, the minutes, the hours, the years that we have been together. All the good moments outweigh the storms. We were in it together. And we thank God, that He kept us and that He is still keeping us today in love. We pray the same for you. Trust in God and put Him first. The best is yet to come!

Mary Ernestine Chance, MDiv

About Monique & Blaine Bailey

Monique Bailey was born in Chester, PA. She is a childcare provider and the author of her first book and memoir, *In My Despair*. Monique has lived most of her life trying to cope with traumatic situations and has now dedicated her life to protecting her two daughters and pastoring with a mission to help others find their deliverance in God.

•

Blaine Bailey was born in Chester, PA and is the oldest of eight siblings. He was raised by his mother in Woodlyn, PA. He graduated from Ridley High School and later finished his education at Pennco Tech, where he studied Auto Body and Mechanical. Blaine graduated with honors.

He has been married for 22 years to his childhood sweetheart and is the proud father of two beautiful daughters.

He is currently the owner of Performance Auto Body and Paint. Bailey faced many obstacles in his life but was able to overcome them by the grace of God. His goal is to do the will of God while maintaining a healthy balance with his family and business.

About Sandra & Leroy Bailey

Sandra (aka Sandy) Bailey is family-oriented and treasures family time with her husband, LeRoy, her two daughters, LaToya and LaTrina, her grandchildren, Brandin Jr., Zara, and Blake, and her mother, Chestina. She spends her free time shopping, traveling and watching television.

•

LeRoy (aka Roy) Bailey is an experienced truck driver of over 30 years and a general contractor, specializing in home remodeling. He is a happy husband to his wife, Sandra, a happy father to his beautiful daughters, and an adoring grandfather to three little ones.

About Mary & Melvin Chance

Mary Ernestine Chance is the oldest of 14 siblings and was born to Richard and Mary Hill, both deceased. She grew up in the area of Tarboro, North Carolina and graduated from Conetoe High School in Conetoe, North Carolina. In 1954, she attended Fayetteville State University for two years. She enrolled in Elizabeth City Teachers College and graduated in 1958 with B.S. in Education and became a teacher at Conetoe High School. She later met Melvin Chance, a loving, devoted man who would become a father to her two precious daughters, Sunny and MiChelle. They married June 2, 1961 and moved to New York and later would have two more loving daughters, Shay and Melva. Over the years, they were blessed with four grandchildren and three great grandchildren, who are the love of their lives. She became a teacher in the New York City Public School System, teaching at several elementary schools and dedicated more than 25 years at P.S. 37 in Queens, New York. She received a Master's in Education from Brooklyn College and a Master of Divinity from New Brunswick Theological Seminary. Mary and her husband joined Calvary Baptist Church in Jamaica, New York and there, founded the Gideonites Prayer Ministry, while Melvin served as a deacon and a member of the Men's Ministry. During this time, she was licensed as an ordained minister through Merrick Park Baptist Church in Queens. After 40 years in New York, they returned to their home in North Carolina and became members of St. James Temple Baptist Church in Tarboro, NC. She is now an associate minister and member of the prayer ministry.

•

Melvin Eugene Chance is the oldest of four siblings born to King Bruce and Bessie Chance. He was born and reared in Martin County, Bethel, North Carolina and graduated from West Martin High School in May 1956. After graduation, he moved to New York and worked for the United States Postal Service. Later, he met the love of his life, Mary Ernestine Knight. She had lost her husband and had two young precious daughters. They dated, fell in love and were married June 2, 1961. They had two beautiful daughters together. He joined Calvary Baptist Church in Jamaica, New York where he served for more than 25 years as a deacon and was a member of the Men's Ministry. He also served as a Worshipful Master in the Masonic Crispus Attucks Lodge No. 60 in New York. After retiring from the United States Postal Service, he and his wife returned to North Carolina in 2001. They attended several churches, and soon joined St. James Temple Baptist Church in Tarboro, North Carolina where Reverend Cornell Joyner is the pastor. He and his loving, devoted wife are still at St. James Temple Baptist Church serving the Lord together. He has served as a deacon since 2002. He's served as a Sunday school assistant superintendent for the past eight years.

About Tanya & Travis Cooley

Tanya Moorehead-Cooley was born and raised in Hartford, CT. During her collegiate career, she attended Johnson & Wales University, University of Connecticut, and the University of Central Florida where she earned her Ph.D. in Exceptional Education. She worked in the Bloomfield Public schools for 7 years as a special education teacher. She is currently an assistant professor at Eastern Connecticut State University. She enjoys spending time with her family, mentoring, working in the community and traveling.

•

Travis L. Cooley, Sr. was born and raised in Erie, PA. He is a graduate of Springfield College where he earned his bachelor's degree in Human Services. He is an Army veteran. He completed a tour of duty in Iraq. He is currently working as a case manager supporting homeless veterans and young adults who are exiting foster care. He is an avid movie goer and enjoys martial arts, time with his family and helping others in need.

The couple met while they lived in Orlando, FL in the summer of 2008. They became friends and later married in 2012. They have a blended family complete with 4 boys and one dog, Trixie. They now live in Bloomfield, CT.

About Patricia & Coley Harris

Patty has more than 25+ years of experience in planning and executing a multitude of memorable events. Patty has brought together her flair for event planning and her entrepreneurial spirit in the form of Patricia D. Harris ~ Hospitality Brokerage Firm, which she's operated for close to 5 years before returning to Corporate America. In March 2014, Patty was recognized by NABFEME's as one of Delaware's Women Trailblazers. In June 2015, she was recognized as a "Mirror" recipient at The Hilton, one of the highest honors given by Meyer & Jabara Management. For two years she served as the Chief Administrative Officer with the Delaware Chapter of the National Association of African Americans in Human where she enjoys being a part of the growing success of the organization. Patty is very active in church and enjoys being a part of the Hospitality Ministry.

●

Coley Harris is a native of Wilmington, Delaware, raised in the Eastlake neighborhood. He has been a youth intervention specialist for 22 years and has worked with adjudicated and non-adjudicated youth through the Nationally Acclaimed Project Aware Program. He has also worked with several Re-entry initiatives, including Strength through Struggle, a released offender support group and the Achievement Center as a volunteer. Coley Harris is the co-founder of Out of the Ashes: where a seed finds life, which is a drama therapy presentation of the reconciliation process between his son, Ahmarr Melton and himself, post incarceration. He is the Lead Research Assistant of the second iteration of the Participatory Action Research project in the city of Wilmington. Coley has co-founded the My Brother's Keeper Mentoring program, which connects young offenders with mentors and positive role models while incarcerated. Most importantly, Coley Harris has a commitment to assisting young people to navigate the pitfalls and the challenges of the street. He uses his life experience to show young people how to manage their feelings of hopelessness, anxiety and apathy.

About Kiara & Pedro Moore

Kiara Moore, MA, LPCMH was born in Pittsburgh, Pennsylvania but now resides in Middletown, Delaware with her family. Kiara is a Licensed Professional Mental Health Counselor serving children, adults and families in the Dover, Delaware area. Kiara treats children in a local middle school and has a private practice, Kiara Moore Therapeutic Services. Kiara received her bachelor's degree from West Chester University of PA, and her master's degree from Eastern University of PA. Kiara is passionate about helping others achieve emotional wellness and resiliency.

•

Pedro Moore is the CEO & Founder of FundingFuel, Inc. He is a seasoned businessman who draws on the lessons and experience he has gained over the course of a successful career in management, venture capital and as an entrepreneur. He has expertise in start-up businesses, entrepreneurship, venture capital investment and directing marketing platforms targeted towards small and mid-sized businesses.

About Tawana & Robert Peterson

Tawana M. Peterson, born native of Hartford, CT on November 24, 1975 to the late Richard L. Hill, Jr. and Bertha D. Holloman Hill. As an undergraduate at Johnson & Wales University, there she met and shortly after became the wife of Robert L. Peterson and with Robert, is now a proud Mother. As a young Wife and Mother, Tawana pursued life as an entrepreneur to help support their family. In doing so, became the owner of Smarty Pantz Early Education Center. Beginning in January 2020, Smarty Pantz Education and Resources (S.P.E.A.R.) will launch its consulting firm for aspiring Early Education Providers. In continued pursuit of supporting Children and Families, Tawana began to advocate for Healthy, Long-lasting

Marriages and is now one of the founders of The Marriage Grit, officially established in August 3, 2018. Although the launching of The Marriage Grit took place in recent years, the mission of supporting and mentoring couples had taken place since the conception of her marriage to Robert in August 3, 1996. Entrepreneurship is life for Tawana as is blood through the veins of her body. Her passion to keep these entities alive is a major priority for her. Tawana has been commissioned to be a light for Human Services and intends on fulfilling this call through everything that she puts her hands to do.

•

Robert L. Peterson is an educator in the Delaware public school system where he holds many roles. He is a Licensed Minister, and Director of Ministries, Entrepreneur and Lecturer. Robert was born in Wilmington, Delaware, and was also educated by the Delaware Public School System. He holds a bachelor's degree in Human Services and a master's degree in Mental Health Counseling, both from Springfield College.

Robert has a keen understanding of the human experience, thus is creative in solution-focused ideals in mentoring and coaching others. Along with Lady Tawana, together, they have founded The Marriage Grit, a network of traditional married couples, created to support the success of each other.

Robert Peterson, M.S. and Tawana Peterson are both professional educators and entrepreneurs. The two have been married for 23 years and share five amazing children. The family resides in the state of Maryland. The Power Couple works to support the Union of Traditional Marriage around the World.

About Candice & William Resto

Candice Resto was born and raised in New Castle, Delaware. Candice has been married to her husband William Resto for over 24 years and they have two beautiful children. Candice holds her Bachelor of Science in Accounting from Wilmington University and currently is employed by one of the largest insurance companies in the U.S. Candice has volunteered as a Girls Scout Leader for over 8 years and serves as the current Pageant Director for Miss Hispanic DE. As with her husband, Candice also volunteers as a Pre-School Coordinator at Faith City Family Church overseen by Past Steve Hare.

•

William Resto Jr. was born and raised in Wilmington Delaware. William has been married for over 24 years and from their union they have two wonderful children, Caitlyn and Brandon Resto. He currently sits on the Board of Directors for the Wilmington Police Athlete League (P.A.L) and Nuestra Raices of Delaware; the organization that annually holds the Wilmington Hispanic Festival and the Miss Hispanic Delaware Pageant. Additionally, he owns and operates, A Bail Bond by Resto & Company and he is the co-founder of the Livingston Resto Project (LRP) a non-profit organization that advocates for the homeless in Delaware. In his spare time, William actively volunteers in the Children's Ministry at Faith City Family Church under the leadership of Pastor Steve Hare for over 20 years. William also is the proud sponsor of the 3 Time Champions "Aquila's" of the Roberto Clemente Little League.

About Christina Watlington & Abdul-Malik Muhammad

Dr. Christina G. Watlington received her doctorate in Clinical Psychology from the University of Maryland, Baltimore County (UMBC) and her bachelor's degree from Franklin & Marshall College. She has over a decade of experience working with clients with depression, anxiety, PTSD and related disorders. She is now the President of a mental health private practice, Dr. Watlington & Associates and the executive director of a not-for-profit organization, Rise & Shine, whose mission is to empower and encourage women to live their best life. Dr. Watlington's hobbies include reading, writing, traveling and spending time with her husband and two amazing children- Sadiki and Ngozi. She is also a member of the American Psychological Association and Delaware Psychological Association. In 2019, she received the Sydney N. Bridgett Award from Franklin & Marshall College for outstanding achievement in her profession.

•

Dr. Abdul-Malik Muhammad has over 20 years serving both youth and adults as a teacher, principal, campus president, executive and state director, and vice president. Dr. Muhammad is always working with the underserved in urban and rural areas. He has focused on the development of Black boys to men, establishing a progressive pedagogy for oppressed youth, and building progressive organizations. Dr. Muhammad also serves as Vice President of several educational, mental health and human services operations in 8 states across the US. Through this work, he continues to diligently work towards transforming lives, one community at a time.

Dr. Muhammad is also actively involved in several national and international organizations, championing an emphasis on Black and Latino youth. Dr. Muhammad holds an Ed.D. in Educational Leadership from the University of Delaware.

AUTHORS
Husbands (in alphabetical order)

Blaine Bailey
LeRoy Bailey
Melvin E. Chance
Travis L. Cooley, Sr.
Coley D. Harris
Pedro Moore
Abdul-Malik Muhammad, Ed.D
Robert L. Peterson, M.S.
Will Resto

CONTENTS
Husband's Side

1   For Better or Worse   130

2   Marriage & Ministry   141

3   In Sickness & In Health   151

4   Blended Families   157

5   Marriage & Infertility   176

6   Interracial Marriage   187

7   Supporting Your Spouse's Dreams   198

8   Marriage & Longevity   206

*   *Poems (appear before every chapter)*

We met in heaven
Tumbled to the wicked earth
Loving, nonetheless

● *Coley D. Harris*

For Better or Worse

1

For Better or Worse
Robert L. Peterson, M.S.

Anyone that has ever attended any sort of traditional wedding ceremony has heard the legendary series of statements, better known as the "wedding vows." Many of us could emphatically recite them simultaneously with either the bride or groom. If we really tried, the majority of witnesses in attendance could create a melody of such, utilizing each member of the wedding party, officiate, bride and groom to create an excellent harmony. The sound would create a beautiful refrain as the wedding officiate would sing the verse while the couple supplied a symphonic response, all while friends, family and well-wishers gesture in excitement, looking forward to the introduction of the new Mr. and Mrs.

Though every person present hears the even exchange of opposites – richer or poor, sickness and in health – I often wonder, how many people in attendance actually listened? What exactly did the preacher say? Was it better or worse, or did they say better and worse? Gosh, I just can't seem to remember, and my father performed mine and Tawana's ceremony. Our summer wedding day in 1996 was full of excitement as we laughed through the light exchange, but I also remember my feelings – *I'm just not prepared for what I'm supposed to do when we leave this sanctuary.* Furthermore, I was terrified and rightfully so – I was only 20! I knew without a doubt that I was madly in love with Tawana, but I was not ready to face the contrary to better.

The most difficult position for a family, is a place of helplessness. The term "family" is utilized in the ideology of a nuclear structure, which suggests that there are two parents and their children. From the perspective of the husband and father in this instance, the challenge is great. I hadn't considered the difficult experiences of marriage.

I often found myself stifled by the same fear experienced on August 3, 1996. Through the years, we would experience various levels of adversity; termination from a career job that I had held for twelve years, while Tawana carried our fifth child. Our first home almost went into foreclosure, we dealt with vehicle repossession, and multiple deaths of close loved ones. The continued struggle was our reality and it became paralyzing. I struggled because I had personally taken the entire weight of our adverse experiences on my shoulders.

Through the years, I would conclude that this was a foolish choice, though it was an honest one, and one often made by most husbands. An intuitive husband is a man who is instinctively conscious of creating success for his family at any cost. After all, I spoke those proud words before God, my soon-to-be bride, and a host of family and friends. I agreed to stand present during the best of times, and even the worst, but for whatever reason, I felt helpless during the moments of struggle.

The struggle of helplessness is a rather profound condition founded in a sense of pride. It is encouraged by embarrassment, coupled with anger, frustration, and internalized doubt. Society has challenged the man to be the lead. Although many fellas willfully accept this challenge, the general expectation is to suppress tears, despise emotion, and strap the family to your back and continue the fight. The theoretic approach of a husband continues to evolve given the time, but the foundation of such remains unchanged – to protect your wife and children. My personal desire as the husband was to encompass the mentioned ideology – to be the superhero, the savior of my family and to protect them from the worst of times, while hoping for better days. However, I would later find that most of the conditions that we would experience as a family had little to do with being a man, but rather just the simple vicissitudes of life. The only way to find resolve and balance would be to reconstruct the mind. In short, I needed to change my way of thinking.

When I think back over the last several years that Tawana and I have been together, I think I was guilty of stressing or overthinking the changes that come with life. Despite that, I always tried to be a practitioner of living in the moment. I had every intent to live one day, one minute and one second at a time. In my mind, there would always be a "better". Even when things were absolutely amazing, deep within my heart of hearts I always felt that it could be "better", but therein lies the problem. Even when things were going rather well, I failed to enjoy the significance of the moment.

On the other hand, one can be physically present, but cognitively elsewhere, never content because of always searching for "better." Several factors exist that impact this process such as immediate family experiences and environment. Men must be mindful of such consideration because each will have an impressionable and profound impact on your ability to be an effective husband and father.

Immediate family experiences and environment factors contribute to one of the most elusive debates known to the psychological community, which is nature vs. nurture. Nature has more to do with the biological implications of a person, things you are born with. Inherited traits from your father, grandfather or mother does contribute to our actions as husbands. Nurture are those contributing external dynamics, such as your associations, such as your friends. Nurture preferences can and often will have a lasting effect on our thoughts and actions toward how we view the responsibilities of a husband. In either case, the implications can either have a positive and/or negative connotation. Men must be mindful of such consideration because each one will often have a profound impact on your ability to be an effective husband and father.

Through the years I would experience the distinct difference between being content and being satisfied. In an earlier point I noted that for me, things could always be better. Although this is true, enjoying every moment is a place of being content. For instance, when Tawana and I rented our first apartment. Although the goal was to purchase a home, moving and living on our own terms was a positive experience that should be enjoyed. Being content is not a final resting place, but rather a moment of planning and preparation for the next step.

On the contrary, satisfaction is a place where vision beyond your current circumstances no longer exists. We could very well have been complacent in the rental of our apartment, never looking beyond the planning process to purchase a home. Ignoring the difference between the terms can cause a level of personal frustration, physical impairment, and socio-emotional impotence. I had concluded that the great majority of situations could easily be described as worse. It was not until I recognized that I was more than enough that things began to change.

Many of our issues are self-inflicted, though I would concede, as mentioned earlier, that family experiences, environment, or general associations also influence our thought processes. It is important to make a definitive decision and take complete control of your own mind. For me, I would create a filter of sorts, in extracting positive influences from negative ones. This procedure is not only difficult, it's necessary. As men, husbands, and fathers, it is important to reveal our individual uniqueness. This process can only be contemplated when we decide to exchange our old way of doing and thinking and search for newfound ideals.

The mind is very intriguing. While it connects the complexities of the body, soul and spirit, it is easily shaken, greeted by the simplicity of a flickering light or a gust of wind. Although easily scattered when task-oriented, man has the innate ability to transform a basic concept into infinite reality. All this may seem complicated, but I can assure you that it is not. The battle is internal rather than competing with an outer force. To fully contemplate being better, we cannot be consumed with the idea of facing worse. Instead, strengthen your mind by overwhelming it with positive reality.

Tawana and I shared the words "I do and I will", or whichever variance of the statement. We also agreed to collaborate through all that was suggested within our vows – for richer, for poorer, for better for worse, in sickness and in health. The key component infused within the ceremony is the term *"we"* which is a distant cry from *"I"*. The understanding of this concept afforded me the opportunity to strategically remove the Superman cape and truly become Clark Kent, further allowing a deeper level of vulnerability I didn't know I could have.

Consider this concept: In order to wholly enjoy marriage, the couple must be willing to appreciate what it means to make love during the day, in the brightness of the light. As jovial as this concept may appear, many couples spend years on end without ever becoming vulnerable. Instead, we are conditioned to make love in the dark, relying only on feeling our way through the experience. With that, we choose to utilize 1/5th of our available senses. Combining all the senses will create not only a more favorable experience, but also something far beyond just a pleasurable outcome. Tawana and I decided that we would spend the rest of our marriage making love in day, meaning we will wholeheartedly accept each other as individuals. As a husband, I am positioned with a newfound strength. I have nothing to hide. Through every moment, for better or worse, I am content and in preparation for the next move.

To become and remain naked and unafraid is not a simple task or for the faint of heart. For the good of the union, I had to get out of my own way and change my way of thinking. I am the head of my family, but I could no longer accept the idea that I was man of steel, emotionless, and afraid to fail. I am a human who is not controlled by my emotions and I can only fail forward. Becoming not only vulnerable for myself and more specifically vulnerable to Tawana, afforded me the opportunity to become the complete man, husband, and father that I am created to be, *for better or worse.*

Robert Peterson, M.S.

It was the moment
That we walked together
In the lowlands,
Where despair had overtaken
The souls of the people,
Heaviness lies upon the hearts
Of the elders and children alike,
She whispered a word
Of love,
And he fed the peoples
Souls,
There was no grand proclamation,
For the work was done
In love and the love
Was for the souls of the people.

                                               • *Coley D. Harris*

Marriage & Ministry

2

Marriage & Ministry
Blaine Bailey

Some would say that I came to God young, but coming from where I came from, we did everything young. I didn't have the luxury of being a normal teenager. Growing up poor, I started selling crack cocaine at 14 and I did what I had to do to survive. At 15, during the summer when I was out of school, I would travel from Woodlyn, Pennsylvania to Chester, Pennsylvania to watch my little cousin, Billy, who was around seven years old while my aunt worked. My aunt was my favorite aunt and so she knew what I was into and I think keeping my cousin was her way of trying to keep me off the streets.

One day while watching my little cousin, he asked me to come to the front door to meet the older sister of one of his friends. I remember Monique coming and peeking through the door and when she saw me, she took off running back towards her house. I was confused because I didn't understand why she had run off, but I found out later that I had caught her off guard and so when she ran, she went to get herself together. I thought that she was cute and she had some hips on her, but her hair was a mess so me catching her off guard had explained the way she looked. Despite the confusion, we ended up hitting it off.

Little did I know that that day I had met someone who would not only become a good friend but who would eventually become my wife. We ended up spending almost every day of the summer together. I was at her house or she was at mine and when we were a part, we would spend countless hours on the phone. We would go to the park for picnics and to feed the ducks, we went to the movies, and a few clubs when her mom would let us borrow the car.

When we were about 17 or 18, Monique recommitted her life to Christ. We tried to continue dating, but I realized that the commitment that she had for God was real and I didn't want to stand in the way of that. We took a break from dating and vowed to remain friends. Oddly enough, it was through her that I was introduced to Christ. I had been to church many times before but this time was different because it was almost as if God had her call me at the time when I was doing some soul-searching and trying to figure out what I was going to do with my life. I started attending church regularly and pursuing my interests - yes, my interests - as in Monique *and* God.

It's interesting because I could remember some years before I would dodge her phone calls because I knew that she would talk about "coming to Christ" and "being saved." I can remember one Sunday, she invited me to church and I sat on the front pew and listened attentively to the message and on occasion, I would glance over at her and think to myself, "Man, she's cute." I later discovered that God does all things well. At the age of 19, I gave my life to Christ and little did I know that God had a plan for my life. As time went on, my love for God grew as well as my love for Monique.

It's funny how things worked out; I started going to church just because I was invited and eventually it became something that I looked forward to doing. It became my happy place, a place where I could go and get joy and be at peace. I especially loved the times when we would travel to places like Savannah, Georgia, which was where our headquarters church was. A few years later, right in Savannah, I was appointed to be a minister and as time went on, I eventually was ordained as an elder of the church. At that point, Monique and I were married and were both called into the ministry.

Over the years, it wasn't always easy being under strict leadership, but somehow, we survive it. Needless to say, I didn't know that there would come a time when I would have to make one of the hardest decisions that I would ever have to make. I allowed my family to attend a church that I was not attending. My wife came to me and expressed that she felt as if she was being spiritual drained and that she was suffering because of a situation that happened in her childhood. I didn't agree with her choice because we were always taught that family should stick together and that the man is the head of his family. I felt that she should've waited for me to make the decision whether to stay or to leave. However, I understood the feelings and the emotions that she was going through since a similar situation happened to me.

I was around 10 years old when I had been mentally and sexually abused. I can remember the situation clear as day. I heard a noise coming from the bedroom and I walked down the hall to see what was going on. I had peeped in on my mom's friend's twenty-something-year-old son, who was my babysitter, to see what the commotion was. With a stern voice, he called me to come into the room. At first, I thought that he was mad that I was peeping in and I remember thinking to myself, "Man, I'm in trouble." As it turned out, he called me into the room to perform sexual acts with a girl who was also in the room, who had to be in her mid-twenties. He instructed me to touch her in different areas of her body and he guided me to have sex with her as she made sounds as if she was enjoying it.

Sexual trauma was something that Monique and I had in common – the only difference was that my abuser was no longer living, and her abuser was a part of the church we fellowshipped in. I know you may ask why wouldn't I leave the church with her? Well, for years Monique and her family had set the tone for the situation, and I was under the impression that they were dealing with this as a family. As time went on, it seemed as though Monique had a hard time dealing with this issue, so we began to talk to one another about it and to my dismay, I found out that what I thought happened was only half the story and there were more sickening details.

To this day, I struggle to imagine the situation and how it played out. Being a man, there are so many scenarios that play out in my head, but being a man of God, I know things can't be handled that way. The reason I remain in fellowship at the church really has nothing to do with rank or position as much as it is about being led by God. Although it may be hard for some to understand, I could relate the situation to when Stephen was stoned, and he prayed for those that stoned him and said, "Lord, forgive them for they know not what they do."

A month or two went by and my family was still attending a different church. Although I went to visit that church from time to time, I knew in my spirit that that was not where God called me to be. It's not that I feel bound to any particular church, but I do feel bound to do God's will and until He tells me what to do, I don't want to make a decision out of pure emotion.

Marriage and ministry are not easy things, but we must realize God did not call us to a life of comfort. I hold to the song, "I Don't Believe He Brought Me This Far to Leave

Me." I would say to any couple trying to be obedient to the call of God that it is important that you do His will, but we must not forget to minister to our partner as well. Praying for one another, uplifting one another, encouraging one another, and being a listening ear are some ways you can minister to your partner. It is my belief that before God gives you revelation for someone else's life, He'll give you revelation for your own life first. There are some things that God has to work out in our lives before we can effectively minister to others.

Years went by and my family continued to fellowship at the church that they attended until one day, my wife approached me and said that she believed that God had called her to pastor her own church. We discussed this matter and I could hear the concern in her voice about what I would say or what my response would be and as she began to ask me how I felt about the situation, I knew that I could not handle it in a fleshly manner. I told her, "If God said it, it will come to pass." In being a minister and trying to do God's will, we must always remember that God's thoughts are not our thoughts, and neither are His ways our ways, so we can't handle a Godly situation in a fleshly manner.

To this day, we are still in different churches, but I support my wife in her endeavors to do God's command. I frequently visit the church that my wife pastors and not only do I visit, but I am there working and helping to build the ministry in any way that I can. I know that God is up to something and in His own time, He will allow us to worship together and build His kingdom as a team. We may not understand what God is doing, but I will continue to pray and ask God for direction concerning ministry and family; after all, the ultimate goal in life is to please God, put Him first, and to do His will.

Blaine Bailey

The better part
Of him is her,
When we talk he recalls
The hard times they endured
with a smile upon his face,
Smoothing over their
Rough edges during
The course of life,
And caring for one another
In their last years.
He says it was love,
Love alone carried them through.

● *Coley D. Harris*

In Sickness & In Health

3

In Sickness & In Health
LeRoy Bailey

A week prior to me having the heart attack, I experienced such an intense pain like never. I was doing some work for my sister at her home in Maryland and had gone to the local lumber store in her town. I remember feeling a pain so sharp and intense in my chest that forced me to stop in my tracks and stand still. My sister witnessed this and became very concerned and wanted to call my wife. I convinced her it was nothing and there was no need to alarm Sandy. I talked it away, figuring it was probably a little gas or indigestion because of how quickly it went away.

I thought I was in the best of health. I could boast that

I was in shape and never had any bad doctor reports. Although I'm diabetic, everything is controlled, and I was consistently told by my doctors to keep up the good work. When you've never been sick before, it is almost unthinkable.

On another note, I was on top of the world regarding my business. I had just landed a potential contract to sign on with a realtor as their contractor for all the homes they would purchase to be "flipped". I was at our dining room table looking over paperwork when I realized I couldn't lift my arms. At that point, I became scared and went into my wife's office, where she was hard at work. I sat in the chair in her office and began to tell her how I was feeling.

That started a snowball effect. We went from her office to the medical aid unit to the ER. Once in the ER, I was greeted by four doctors of which two were surgeons that quickly explained I was having a heart attack and they needed to get me to surgery right away.

Was I really hearing these words?! If so, how could that be? I thought I was a dead man. I remember talking the entire time as they partially put me out while they were performing the procedure. I lost all sense of time. I couldn't tell you how long anything took. All I know is I started to look back over my life. I was in a space of thinking I was dead, and my prayer was that everyone left behind would be alright.

When Sandra and I got married and had children, I asked the Lord to let me live long enough to see them graduate. Once that happened, I thanked the Lord for giving me that and then I asked to live long enough to see my grandchildren. Toya, my oldest daughter, was pregnant with our first grandchild at the time, so I figured the Lord didn't grant me my last desire and had taken me home. The first set of medication they gave me had me in an in-between state, and I was given meds after the procedure was over that totally knocked me out. When I woke up later, I realized I didn't die and had survived the heart attack.

I was still somewhat relaxed and giddy, when suddenly, my wife became ill and had to be taken to the ER from my room. I didn't fully realize what was going on with her until the next day. When I realized what happened to her, my anxiety set in all over again. Now, I was thinking that *she* was going to die. I remember feeling so low, empty and confused. What was I going to do without the best part of me? How was I going to be able to go on? Was it my fault she had the stroke? Will the girls blame me? So many questions and thoughts ran through my head, but when I saw her and she convinced me she was going to be okay, I was better.

It was strange going home from the hospital and leaving her there, especially since I was initially the one with the major issue. I tell you, things can change in a moment and we can never expect it.

Once Sandra came home, I thought things would be back to normal, but I had hurdles ahead of me that I had never imagined. The medicines I had to take because of my heart attack came with a lot of side effects. My doctor tried preparing me for some of them but until you go through them, it's unimaginable. The depression and suicidal thoughts were overwhelming. I sat day by day and felt like I was continually falling down a well and there was no way out for me, but I am here to tell you that almost five years later, I am still here by the grace of God and looking forward to as many more years as He will allow. I not only got to see my first grandchild be born, but I've lived to see all three wonderful, beautiful, healthy, and thriving grandchildren enter this world. Through it all, I'm just happy to be alive and to be sharing life with my best friend, my wife.

LeRoy Bailey

And so they found that
Love was abundant,
Overflowing from their union
Traditions melded and
Customs were redefined,
A new clan rising,
Forged through tears
And solidified with
Authenticity
No longer separate
But one,
And in this oneness
The children laugh
And play,
For all that they have ever known
is family.

● *Coley D. Harris*

Blended Families

4

Blended Families
Travis L. Cooley, Sr.

I had kids when I was young, so I knew a blended family was inevitable if I ever wanted to get married after my relationship with my children's mother, "Jane" (a pseudonym used to protect her privacy), ended. We overcame some difficult times in our youth as a couple and as parents. We had a strong connection before and after our relationship. We were friends and supported each other, which is why I assumed my potential blended family would not be difficult to establish.

Obstacles

To understand my story, it is important to explain the

obstacles that Jane and I faced as a young, African American couple living in a racist and oppressive community with minimal opportunities for the growth and financial stability needed to raise our children.

A few weeks after 9/11, my first son was born. A week after that, I laid in a pool of my blood on the ground in handcuffs, half dead after being beaten by racist cops. My name was all over the place, in at least 100 newspapers. The people I stood next to in uniform not only left me hanging but beat me down even more.

The military was all I had. 1st 112th Infantry Division out of Erie, Pennsylvania had already been on the racist train and that case just gave them ammunition to disown me. They used the "N" word freely. They called my mother's house, being disrespectful on her answering machine. Between 2001 to 2005, I served in the Army National Guard for free because someone stole my uniform from my locker, and I had to pay for it. I still served with my dignity intact, but I never got my ranks and the awards I deserved.

One year later, my second son was born. Although we had no support system – no help from family, friends, or our community, Jane and I worked hard for our children and always wanted the best for them. The only person who showed up for us was my sister, Jessica, who shared her time and her love and even forced me to take money when we needed it. I am grateful for her being in our lives, supporting us through some of the most difficult times and the great moments I hold closest to my heart. Nothing would stop us from giving our kids a better life and being present for them. We were two kids who did not have anyone and were holding on to each other for dear life.

I was railroaded in the court case that ended in 2005. To this day, I still never got to say what actually happened that night. Some lawyer who I interviewed with and decided to not go with called me one day. He said, "Travis, you got a warrant for your arrest. If you meet me at the courthouse, I can help you clear it up. I don't want you to get jammed up," he said.

I met him at the courthouse, and Judge Ernest DiSantis was happy to see me because he assumed I signed a plea deal. He stated how it was a good move so we could get on with this case, but I stopped him because I never agreed to plea to anything. The judge got very upset and began rambling about how "this thing had gone on long enough."

He showed me the plea with a signature that was *not* mine. They gave me a court-appointed attorney who reeked of liquor and cigars who knew very little about my case. I was hardly prepared, but in just a short time, the jury found me not guilty of all charges. The difficult judge decided to overturn some of the charges and charged me with a misdemeanor and a summary offense, resulting in a sentence of a year probation, 25 hours of community service, and hundreds of dollars in fines.

The final nail in the coffin for me was during one Memorial Day weekend that involved me firing a warning shot with my legal firearm that the same police officers that jumped me arrested me for. I got trumped-up charges that added up to 14 years in prison. This time I found my own lawyer, but he was in with all the wrong people in town. He offered me a deal; if I dropped the case and took $20,000, the charges would be dropped. I signed right then and there and as soon as I handed him the signed document, he handed me a check for only $11,000. I stared at him for about 10 seconds, turned around, and walked out of there. Only a few days after making sure my kids had all the clothes, school supplies, bikes, and whatever else I could think of, I left town never to return and drove to Las Vegas to start a new life.

I had to leave because my military career tanked. I could barely find a job anywhere because of the high-profile case, so against my will, I left without my kids in order to feed them and stay alive and free for them.

Everyone who lives in Erie understands that it is truly a different world. Erie is one of the worst parts of America. Black people were discriminated against without consequences, black culture was demeaned and looked down on, and the KKK could roam freely and terrorized black neighborhoods with police escorts.

Jane and I survived the Mississippi burning case on top of surviving in broken homes, so we knew we could survive anything. We promised each other, regardless of whoever came into our lives or obstacles we faced, we would always stay connected and remain a united family for our children, whom we love dearly and wanted nothing but an abundance of love, laughter, and victory. My kid's mother had supported my efforts in trying to find a way out of the madness we were raised in and around. No matter how outrageous they were, we both agreed that we would try anything. She did not want to leave with me for other family-related reasons, but she knew I needed to and why.

Making Changes

I stopped hanging out late, started praying more and drinking less. I stopped hanging out with everyone who I hung out with before. I broke up with women I dated who wouldn't be a good fit for my children. I stopped buying music with explicit lyrics and language because I cared about what came out of my mouth and what my boys would hear me say. I read more, wrote more, and exercised more. I buried my ego and sharpened my self-esteem and character so much that I became a new person. Though I wasn't perfect, I wanted to make sure everything was right so when my boys looked at their dad, they would see a man that they might want to become. Sadly, I was mistaken.

Our blended family was not set up by me, but by God – I merely prayed for the woman that I have in my life and she has rearranged my world. Tanya loves everyone, but she especially loves my boys just as much as I do. She has thought of things I would have never imagined helping us through the most difficult times, and I am grateful. She has dealt with and witnessed the confusion, frustration, and depression. I have had some intense life experiences, but this one has tested my will and ultimately has brought me closer to God. I knew God had a sense of humor when I'd bang my head on the corner of an open cabinet door or trip over my own two feet when I imagined giving up on our blended family. I experienced God's love by getting a little time with my kids and dreaming about them when I didn't see them. Some dreams would make me laugh and others would make me cry, but I appreciated every moment.

I have gotten upset and impatient with God because of the lesson he has hidden within this whole blended family situation. It has been such a long roller coaster ride that I kind of don't want to know the rest because I'm exhausted. I trust God, but I'm still upset, hurt, and tired. However, I refuse to believe God has taken me through these flames for nothing.

Our Wedding

When Jane found out I was getting married, she did not want the kids to be a part of our wedding or family. She wouldn't even allow them to be in or come to the wedding. Unfortunately, she never got onboard. It was my wife's idea to recreate a ceremony. Tanya and I agreed that love and inclusion were our only options. Thanks to her and my sister's persistence and efforts, our boys were able to visit.

They came to our home when we lived in New Jersey

and then in Connecticut several times. We had a ball each time; we went to the water park, the arcade, the movies, and raced bumper cars. We showed them around Connecticut and introduced them to their extended family and our friends. We let them know that our home was their home. Things got bumpy sometimes with the attitudes and the loyalty towards their mother. The kids were obviously not sure if they were "allowed" to love us or have fun with us.

When we saw the change in attitude and the misbehavior from the boys, we tried something different and way outside of all our comfort zones. We invited Jane down to hang out with us many times, but she never accepted. When we did speak to Jane about arranging the boys' departure, there was very little conversation. She was not involved in helping to repair a relationship that she was destroying between father and sons. We did things to avoid further separation and the destruction of our blended family and even went to therapy. I had many conversations with both my sons about the relationship between a father and son and the expectations we all had for them. Being a kid was the main expectation because for some strange reason they worried about adult things at an early age like child support, court hearings, and custody.

My oldest son, Travis Jr., got very difficult. Hell, he wanted to change his name when he was eight years old. Travis Jr. gave me and my wife, his brother, his teachers, and even the summer camp we sent him to a hard time and eventually, I had to chastise him. I can't say that the spanking he got changed his ways, but after that, he acted differently and for the better. He went from acting stank and ungrateful to having instant gratitude and became a model student.

When the kids got home with Jane, I did not even get a phone call from her saying the kids made it home safely and everything was fine. I called and texted almost every day for months, but not too much because I had to continue to walk on eggshells to see my kids. She finally texted me saying that she was cutting all communication between me and the kids and that she did not think it was a good idea that me and her spoke on the phone either. I filed a contempt of court but had to drop it because the courts said I had to file in person.

Right after that, Jane filed for full custody. The only way I could defend it was in person and I could not make it because I started a new job. I followed the procedure to notify the court why I could not make it and I entered my defense which included a plea to have my boys in my life more because there was no supervision or anyone raising them. I had been tracking them through school since the beginning. The teachers and counselors were the only way I could get information about my kids' wellbeing, progress, condition and attitudes. My concerns and my guarantee of results fell upon deaf ears in Erie courts. Their goal had been to separate fathers from their households ever since their factories closed. The town could only survive on the penal system and the failure and separation of black families and other families of color. They couldn't even pay the teachers and keep the schools open. A few years later, I would watch my kids' grades tank and my oldest smoke weed on his new Facebook account that myself and wife were blocked on.

Because I could not make it, the judge took away all the visitation we had fought for years for. It was a dramatic change in all our lives that did more harm than good. The first time in over a year I heard from my kids' mom was in court. She told the judge I was crazy, on drugs, and was an unfit parent. I addressed her right then and there and expressed my disappointment in her for not having one conversation with me until that point. I did not care who was in the room; I made the lawyer be quiet because he obviously did not care about what that meant for our boys and he surely did not understand the struggle and barriers for young black boys in that severely impoverished, heavily racist town. Still, we accomplished nothing. I got depressed and fell into a funk that impacted my house and the pregnancy and birth of my first son with my wife. I felt like I could not be a father to the new kids until I was a father to the kids that were already here. The bonding phase was rough for me and Ethan, but we made it. The process affected our marriage and still sometimes does. I didn't feel like the great man, father, and husband I dreamed of being when I was young.

Jane was very vocal about not wanting my wife involved in any court proceedings or conferences as soon as Tanya and I got married. My wife had more experience than the two of us combined in raising kids in a stable home without children. Jane and I had never even seen a stable home, especially with both parents. My wife was and had been active in her church since she was a child, was a Ph.D. professor of special education, an excellent example of a mother, stepmother, wife, mentor, mediator, and so much more. I was embarrassed that Jane would behave that way and towards the kids' stepmom. We couldn't even convince her to let the kids take our calls on their birthdays. It wouldn't be long before the relationship we established and reestablished with our boys would once again become a memory.

I last saw them when they were 12 and 13 years old. I didn't know that we wouldn't see or hear from them again until my boys were young men – 17 and 18 years old to be exact. The first time I laid eyes on my baby boys was Christmas of 2018, almost five years later. It felt so good seeing them; I was happy and completely shocked at how big they had gotten. I was on the verge of crying, somewhat disappointed and a little upset with how much I had missed out on after trying to do right by them.

During the years that were gone, I had visions of past moments and vivid dreams of us having normal conversations or us laughing together, like the flashbacks people supposedly get before they die. I suppose I felt like a piece of me was dying every time I had a vision or dream and because of this, I began to change. Things were not as funny as they used to be, and I was not as likely to say yes to things I used to love doing.

Tanya and I did our best to include them in our family, despite all the obstacles that stopped us from connecting. I told them I wanted them to live with us, but it was up to them to decide. They wanted some time to think about it, but they claimed they wouldn't mind. That was enough for me. We immediately began claiming space and rooms to make this transition work. I took them to my boring job, they met a few of my clients and my coworkers. We talked about karate, Erie, and family members on their mom's side that I considered family too. I found out that their grandmother, "Big Momma," had passed away, their uncle was in jail for a long time, and other sob stories about people I grew up with and around before my sons were born. I expressed how disappointed I was that nobody told me that these things happened in the family. I shared stories with them about the visits and holidays Jane and I spent at her grandmother's house, and how me and Jane's family had a lot a fun with silly dance offs, games, and partying when we all were kids. I think it was then that they realized that I loved them and the people around them too.

My boys still know nothing about me or how much I love them. I feel like I am naturally failing as a man and a father no matter what I do or accomplish because two human beings in this world are being misinformed about where they come from. They did not even know that they were both born in Erie at Hampton Hospital in the early mornings of their birthdays.

All that time we missed out on was because Jane made crazy claims in court. I hadn't seen or spoken to her in years, but just recently, she had a sudden change of heart. She now believes that the best place for my kids is with me. She claimed they need my love, my wisdom, and support. I went from being a "dead-beat dad" who didn't love his kids to being the best example of a man and father that my boys needed.

She admitted that she told the kids she is the reason they hadn't seen us all that time and that she is the one that fought in court to keep them away from me. I felt like she did the worst possible harm that anyone can do to their children besides abandon them, which is sad because we were both abandoned by our parents. I know she felt the sting from being tossed to the side because I was with her every step of the way and after. Thankfully, through all of that, we have seen the boys, but even with a strong foundation, a loving family, and a village, the boys have not spent as much time with us as we would have liked. They now have a five-year-old and a two-year-old brother who think they are rock stars and look up to them despite not being able to see them much.

I do not want my boys to grow up not knowing who they are or where they come from. I do not want them confused, angry, or thinking something is wrong with them. I don't want them to have regrets or be jealous of their younger brothers or anyone else. I want them to understand. I will put my all into raising my younger sons. They will naturally have more opportunities growing up because they have both parents and a village fighting for them, protecting them and advising them. It is exactly what we have been begging my oldest sons to be a part of all these years. Now, we can only pray that with some listening and understanding, we can build a better future together.

I've made peace with the situation and within myself and I am moving on. Though very rough, and at times hopeless, I can still love my boys from afar and live my life. My other sons need to see a whole man in front of them, not a broken father. God asked me to step aside long ago and I have. I still try though. My door swings both ways for my boys, but I have to live too.

What I Wanted It to Be

I wanted my boys to love us all as we love them. I assumed that the adults would sit down and reflect on the obstacles that our kids would face and do our best to protect and eliminate the unnecessary challenges. I hoped that our holidays would be spent together with Jane on the team. I prayed that my two oldest sons would engage with my two youngest and be the positive influences and brothers that we all knew they were.

What It Is

My predictions about what could happen are coming true. I expected that they would forget about us and lose interest in the things they used to love. The same thing happened to me and my brother, and I did not want that for them. I wanted them to have a chance to be kids before they started worrying about adult problems.

My Hope

I hope that they will communicate with us and visit. I want them to grow up and be loving, caring, protective, and responsible young men. I want the best for them, even if it does not include us.

Tips to Consider

If anyone stands in the way between you loving and being there for your kids, fight from the beginning to the end. Tell the truth, and don't sugarcoat anything. Mothers, if you are keeping kids from their dad, own it, say why, and give the dad the chance to explain and redeem himself. Let him raise his kids, even if you don't like him anymore.

Take any and every opportunity you can to see and talk to your kids regularly. Show up for them and make them get used to seeing you.

No matter how tough circumstances become, be a united front. Stand together for the kids through every situation. Stand together when you have fallen and when it's time to plan for the future. When it is time to celebrate victory, do it together. Do not exclude one another because of conflict, what someone else may think, or new relationships and do not exclude yourselves. Togetherness will be your strongest ally if you all work towards it together.

Last but not least, keep God first in everything you do. A family that prays together, stays together. Always think about the future, the bigger picture of your blended family, and the greatness your families will bring and leave behind.

Travis Cooley, Sr.

*In the still hours
He often wonders,
Never questioning God
Yet mourning
for what could never be.
Yes,
It is in the still hours
That he wonders.*

● *Coley D. Harris*

Marriage & Infertility

5

Marriage & Infertility
Pedro Moore

My name is Pedro Moore. I am a serial entrepreneur and venture capitalist, and I was blessed to marry my gift from God, Kiara Moore, on May 21st, 2011.

When I was in middle school, I prayed to God for a brown-skinned woman with a nice body, an amazing face, who was around 5'5", and a virgin and God delivered by the time I was 26 years old. I had recently gotten out of a relationship and, at the time, Kiara was single, so our pastor hooked us up. He used the excuse that he wanted us to work on a "project", but in reality, it was just an excuse for him to get us together and it worked! The interesting thing about our relationship was that there was no period of "courting". Our first date as a couple, despite neither of us asking each other to be officially boyfriend and girlfriend, was in October of 2009. We hit it off so well, that without saying, we both considered ourselves a couple on the very first date. I believe we both just knew, and we went forward. After two months, I told her I loved her. After six months, I proposed. One year later, we got married.

The beginning of the marriage was great, though there were some learning curves, and we both had to adjust to each other as in any marriage. My vision for our family was that I would be a wealthy business owner, which would allow us to afford a nice home, have several kids, and Kiara could be a stay-at-home wife. I thought the most difficult part of that vision would be owning a business or maybe figuring out how to live with each other. I never thought it would be having children, especially with the fact that I was in my late 20s, but when the time came for us to plan our family, we found out that we would have major obstacles to face.

After experiencing infertility personally, I now realize it is very common but not widely discussed amongst peers. It is as if it is an embarrassment not to be able to have children naturally like everyone else. So many individuals suffer from infertility. According to the NICHD Information Resource Center, studies suggest that after one year of having unprotected sex, 12% to 15% of couples cannot conceive, and after two years, 10% of couples still have not had a live-born baby. As a kid, without realizing the seriousness of the matter, you make fun of the infertility issues not realizing that infertility could be an issue that you face in your adult years.

I felt helpless, but as a result of the news, we had to be intimate more frequently to increase our chances of success. However, it was difficult and not always pleasurable because in the back of my mind I knew it wouldn't work and often questioned why we were doing it. It is like being in the gym, working on your jump shot but you keep missing, shooting bricks. It feels as if things would never get better, so it was pointless to try. Many told me, "Don't worry about that, just enjoy the intimacy," but I still struggled to do that because my real motivation was to increase the chances of pregnancy and the doctors clearly stated we could not have kids naturally. I could not help wanting to give up. It became harder for me to be intimate, but I had to get past the apprehension and trust in God.

Difficulties in life can bring tension into any relationship, whether intentional or not, and marriages are no exception. As we were going through this challenge of infertility, we also lost several loved ones within two years, including Kiara's only brother. Kiara and I definitely loved each other, but the circumstances caused both of us to run low on patience and our home life was not pleasant. How can two be intimate with each other if there is friction between the two? It was not easy, but prayer, faith, and consistency had to be present. Here are three tips that helped us through that difficult time and strengthened our love for each other.

- *Have faith*; this may seem cliché, but it is true and let's be honest, it is easier said than done. Why? As a human, it is hard to see the light at the end of the tunnel when it is completely dark. However, according to Hebrews 11:1 (KJV), "*Now faith is the substance of things hoped for, the evidence of things not seen.*" The whole point of faith is having a positive outlook even though the odds are stacked against you because you know Christ will see you through. Having faith consists of two parts, 1) deciding to believe in Christ and that he will bring you through your situation and 2) believing Christ through your actions, because faith without works is dead

(James 2:17). How can a person believe they will become a millionaire when their actions show otherwise? Instead of building a business, that person lies on the couch watching Netflix all day. Though they say they plan to be a millionaire, they don't really believe it. If you truly believe in something, even though it hasn't manifested yet, you will move forward as if it has and patiently wait for it to catch up. That is faith. God said you only had to have faith as big as a mustard seed. We have doubts and we may shift back and forth in belief, but we must stand strong on the Word of God by studying the Bible and talking to Him. We forget to talk to him, but this is a reminder to keep the dialogue with God open. Let Him know you are having doubts or that you are feeling discouraged. Do things to prepare for the miracle. The doctors ran test after test and concluded that we could not have a child naturally, which hurt the both of us. Doubt and sorrow really began to sink in, and we didn't think we would ever have any kids. We eventually got ourselves together and started believing. We put our faith into action by buying pampers and getting the room ready because we just believed that one day, we would have a little one.

- I believe that when going through life's challenges, one way to help you get through is by helping others that are going through a similar challenge. As the bible says, *"It is more blessed to give than to receive,"* (Acts 20:35, KJV). Sometimes we forget that we are not the only ones in the world that have problems and that God may want us to touch other individuals that may be going through. Because someone prayed over us and we bought diapers to sow the seed into the miracle, we wanted to pay it forward. We bought a pack of diapers and had our first lady of our church anoint and pray over the box of pampers. Then, we wrote a note for each diaper and mailed them out to our friends who were having difficulty having kids. We are happy to report as of today, four out of our eight friends either had a baby or are currently pregnant.

- *"The scary prayer"* – what is it? It is when you ask God if this prayer request is in his will and if not, to please remove the want. That prayer is hard to ask because you really want your desire fulfilled. However, I thank God that he knows the beginning from the end. Kiara and I appreciate God for unanswered prayers because it wouldn't have led us to where we are today. As a believer, the Bible teaches you, *"In everything, give thanks."* (I Thessalonians 5:18, KJV). Whatever the outcome, we still have to praise God and appreciate who he is and what he has done for us despite the results. That's love. We don't want friendships with conditions like *if you give me what I want, we can remain friends.* No, we want someone to remain a friend no matter what. When my wife and I received the heartbreaking news from multiple doctors that we would not be able to have kids naturally, it devasted us. There were moments we wanted to throw in the towel, but we prayed that prayer. God told us to trust the process, and we had to accept the fact that His will supersedes ours.

On our 6th wedding anniversary, May 21, 2017, Kiara surprised me with the best gift ever. She was pregnant and the way she surprised me was great. The day before, May 20, 2017 at 11:59pm, Kiara woke me out of bed, screaming that I had to come downstairs to open my anniversary gift. In my mind, I thought she was tripping because we could have waited later in the day to open the gifts, however, she insisted, so I did. As I opened the package, I kept noticing all these dad references, but I was a little slow in "catching it" until I saw the pregnancy test with the positive mark.

Overwhelmed with joy, I just cried. I was a little confused though because the doctors stated that we could not have kids naturally, so how could this happen?

When it came time to do a baby announcement, I told Kiara that we couldn't just do a regular announcement. We had to do an announcement that spoke to what we had gone through. While waiting on our miracle baby, three family members passed away and during the time, one of our favorite TV shows, *A Different World*, gave us peace. So, we reenacted the scene where Whitley tells Dwayne that she was pregnant, and we used that scene to transition into our personal journey of beating infertility. Our baby announcement video went viral, hitting 60K+ views, 400+ shares, and almost 500 comments. We even received comments from the actual celebrities from that show, such as Sinbad, Kadeem Hardison, who played Dwayne, and Cree Summer. To top it all off, we received a lot of messages from various individuals sharing their personal stories. The outpour and support we received from the people suffered from the same issue we had was overwhelming.

The day came, January 27, 2018, when Winston T. Moore arrived and I was excited but also extremely scared, as I knew nothing about raising children. I was completely clueless, but I was so happy. I felt like a proud father and so many visions for his future came to mind. I was just so excited. I held him every chance I could, changed diapers, fed him and did anything I could do to spend time with him.

Here is the reality: everyone's journey will be different. There will be cases where some parents will have kids naturally, there will be cases where some will have to use in vitro fertilization (IVF) and there will be cases where some will have to adopt. The bottom line is that we must be happy with God's will and realize that there was a reason for this outcome. The outcome does not determine the quality of you being a parent or a great person. You are not less than because your peers have a different route than you. Remember, love is important between you and your spouse. With that main ingredient, you will get through any situation.

Pedro Moore

In our own skin
Loving one another fiercely
Challenging the world
Honoring our past
Creating an eternity
I see you for you,
And together we are.

● *Coley D. Harris*

Interracial Marriage

6

Interracial Marriage
William Resto

In the mid-90s, interracial marriages were considered a bit of an anomaly, but what does God's word say about it?

The bible never says that interracial marriage is wrong; anyone who hinders interracial marriages is doing so without biblical authority. As Martin Luther King, Jr. noted, "a person should be judged by his or her character, not by skin color." There is no place in the life of a Christian for favoritism based on race. In fact, the biblical principle is that there is only one race – the human race – with everyone having originated from Adam and Eve. Our belief is that faith in Christ, not skin color, is the scriptural standard for choosing a spouse.

Thus, it's all about God's word. The beauty of this is a grace-transcending gospel that we are all made in His image, all made equally the same. I believe that our marriage is a reflection and a representation of what we all are in store for in heaven. All different races coming together, united as one, praising our Lord and Savior, Jesus Christ.

In the beginning

I grew up on the westside of Wilmington, Delaware, a predominately Puerto Rican neighborhood in the late '70s, early to mid-80s. My family had strong family ties within the Puerto Rican community. My grandparents, Luis and Lucy Sierra, were one of the first Puerto Rican families to migrate to the city of Wilmington. I would be remised if I did not mention that my uncle, Anthony Resto, who was the first highest elected official in the great State of Delaware became the first Puerto Rican councilman in the 5th District in the city of Wilmington back in 1972.

My first encounter with the future Mrs. Resto

The opportunity to meet my wife presented itself in the mid-90s. It was a midafternoon, summer day when my sister, Aida, asked me to call her place of employment to let them know that she was running a little behind. If my memory serves me well, I believe she was running late due to picking up some rice and beans my mother had just made. Anyway, I called her job and unbeknownst to me I was speaking to my future wife. Of course, me being the person I was, I began flirting with her in my Barry White "show you right" voice. That didn't seem to work at first, but I remained steadfast in my pursuit and did not take no for an answer.

The Courtship of the Future Mrs. Resto

She truly played hard to get. I really had to put in hard work and I'm glad that I did because of His promise… *"For I know the plans I have for you," declares the Lord, "plans to prosper you and not to harm you, plans to give you hope and a future."* (Jeremiah 29:11)

The beauty of growing up on the westside of Wilmington was that I never saw the color of one's skin as an issue; however, this is when we started to see some kickback from other minority groups. We got more pushback from the black community only because if you didn't know me, your first impression would have been, "Why is this sistah with this white boy", not realizing that I was a minority just like the person making the statement.

The big moves of '95, the Engagement & the Elopement?

By this time, we were going steady and I couldn't stop thinking about her nor could I wait to see or hear her voice. It was early 1995; we decided to move in together and within a couple weeks, I knew I wanted to spend the rest of my life with Candice M. White. We decided to fly out to Las Vegas to elope. We got married on August 17th, 1995 and we knew that on our first anniversary, we wanted to renew our vows not only before God, but our families. Even though we decided to renew our vows in a church near home, I still could not muster the strength to attend churches with my newly wedded wife. It was a true struggle for me.

By this time, the struggle between my earthly desires and wanting to escort my wife to church was real. I can recall a time when I got enough guts to finally attend a friend's church in Chester, Pennsylvania, but I let my wife down once more. When we arrived at the church, for some reason, I couldn't go inside; it was as if a huge weight was place on me and my nerves took over. My wife simply said, "okay," and off I went to visit my aunt and cousins that also lived in Chester.

In January 1996, a co-worker of mine, Alfonzo, invited me to a men's conference at his church, Union Baptist Temple in Bridgetown, New Jersey. I remember this day like it was yesterday; I meet his pastor, Albert Morgan, and he told me that he has been hearing a lot about me and my struggles and asked if I would do him the honor of eating at his table for lunch. The icebreaker question that he asked me jokingly was, "Rice and Beans or Spaghetti?" He knew I was Puerto Rican, but he couldn't tell because I looked Italian. I must admit that the experience was truly the most remarkable and memorable experiences that I have ever encountered in my life. The only downside to that experience is that it ended too soon. It seemed as though each speaker touched me in ways only God knew because I never discussed my past with anyone. Brother Alfonzo and Pastor Morgan will always have a special place in my heart for assisting me in beginning my spiritual walk with God. Thank you, brothers in Christ!

Searching for a home church

One would think this would be an easy task to accomplish, however, this was probably one the hardest tasks to take on as a babe in Christ. As the head of my household, I had to ask myself difficult questions like should my household begin practicing Roman Catholic? Do we convert over to Pentecostal or even Baptist? Did I mention that my wife's father, Jerome Beck, was a pastor? During this life changing moment in time, our daughter was about to come into this world, and we didn't want to push a conventional religion on her. Over some time, we visited many churches, some of which made us uncomfortable until we were led to attend a non-denominational church.

"Unequally Yoked"

Unfortunately, individuals have been misinterpreting the Scripture for centuries about being unequally yoke.

I know this is a bit cliché, but when I met my wife in May of 1994, it was love at first sight. She was the turning point of my life because I was so into this world, running the streets and involved in things I shouldn't have been into… but God. God's grace and mercy saved me, but it was through my wife's ministry, unbeknownst to us, that started the transformation process in my life, changing me into the man I am now. I like to call it "the ministry of a wife's unconditional love" and I'm reminded of a Scripture that provides clear instruction to those married to unbelievers. However, let me just clarify something here – it's not that I wasn't a believer. I was raised in a predominately Puerto Rican neighborhood where everyone was a Roman Catholic and we all attended St. Paul's Catholic Church, where we went to church every Sunday, Wednesday and sometimes on Saturdays. In some church services, I even served as altar boy – go figure. However, as I got older, I just wasn't a "practicing Catholic" anymore. Peter wrote the following:

"If any woman has a husband who is an unbeliever, and he consents to live with her, she should not divorce him. For the unbelieving husband is made holy because of his wife, and the unbelieving wife is made holy because of her husband. Otherwise your children would be unclean, but as it is, they are holy." (1 Corinthians 7:13-14).

Scripture vaguely approaches the "how to" of traveling through the journeys of interracial marriage, however scripture does speak explicitly about the ministry potential of unequally yoked spouses. In this case, I was the unbelieving husband who was made holy because of a Proverbs 31:10-31 woman!

I did not get a pass to enjoy salvation indirectly through my wife but rather that closeness to my wife's Christ-centered living manifested opportunities for me to receive more godly inspiration through her unwavering love for me. Therefore, every time your wife reveals these characteristics to you, it's just another opportunity to be affected by the godlessness that wishes to assert itself into our soul. In this way we are "made holy" because he is set apart from the world and more likely to receive the gospel.

Because we have kept the family unit intact for the last 24 years, our children, our family, our community will have a greater chance to witness this revelation and to be more understanding to these spiritual and biblical truths.

I believe these assurances on marriage and especially between unequally yoke spouses written prophetically to the church are not simply reference points but timeless blessings that are words of wisdom that apply even more today. Choosing to stay in this relationship provided me the opportunity to minister to my believing spouse, aiding in the rebuilding process between our spiritual connections. By no means can we change the person we are married to even if we wanted to. However, we can only work on becoming the person God intended us to be and only then will we realize who we were called to be in the Lord and appeal to God's grace and mercy.

I've witnessed this in my own transformation in various ways and in different areas over the last 24 year of blissful marriage. As a couple, we decided to attend a non-denominational church, Faith City Family Church, and to try to live the lives that Jesus lived, one with an attentive heart that avoids the influences of resentment, aggravation, and disturbance. My wife has the ability to soften the hardest of hearts. We as husbands miraculously transform from natural to the spiritual. What I have learned over these past 24 years is that we are called to be faithful to the Scripture of our Lord and Savior, Jesus Christ despite our circumstances and individual short falls.

In conclusion, interracial marriage is not a matter of what's right or wrong but a unity of wisdom, discernment and prayer, for we are a powerful illustration of our equality in Christ.

William Resto

She dreams in color
And I watch quietly,
Gathering her canvases
And brushes,
Placing her paints
Near at hand.

● *Coley D. Harris*

Supporting Your Spouse's Dreams

7

Supporting Your Spouse's Dreams
Abdul-Malik Muhammad, Ed.D.

Power couple. We hear that a lot and it makes us smile that special smile that couples have when they know a secret about themselves that others don't. Usually, folks are looking at the level of success Christina and I have had in our businesses or raising our family. Yes, we are proud of that, but for us, the power comes not in what we get credit for out in the world, but from how we lean into each other, believe in each other, and celebrate both the big and small accomplishments.

Our love story was part *Love and Basketball* without the basketball, part *Love Jones* without the poetry and mostly

Brown Sugar without the hip-hop mogul part. In other words, we were two young Black kids who knew there was something special in the other at first sight. She was more than fly and it only took me just half a minute to realize that she was also brilliant, compassionate, and funny in the most stunning way. To her credit, she was able to look past the grit and big talk to see the real me – a vulnerable, young man trying to understand himself and his place in the world. Our relationship began during our sophomore year in college. Our first pregnancy came quickly, but we got our feet underneath of us, got married, and launched into the dynamic balance of family, work, and school. It was then that we learned our first important lesson – accept that your partner is always in a process of "becoming".

The idea of "becoming" is a popular one now thanks to Michelle Obama's bestselling book, but maybe not so much back in the early 90s for a barely-out-of-their-teens married couple. Not only were we still changing physically and emerging into adulthood, but we were becoming something radically different than our friends and what our families sent us to college for. During those first years, I witnessed Christina become a young mother, fiercely determined to model how a woman sets her mind to a dream and succeeds for our new daughter. She was also becoming more aware of her own powerful voice, nurtured by our tribe of activist mentors and comrades. I was also becoming more human, settling into the realization that the world is less black and white and full of an interesting range of complex ideas and that I didn't have the best ones.

As we look back at our journey, the idea of "becoming" is a central but easy one for us to see. We met and married at a time in our development when change was the norm. The world, politics, our geography, size of family, jobs as well as mindsets, friendships, physical features and hopes have all evolved or outright changed over these years. We've embraced the notion that we are perfectly imperfect on this journey and we love each other through it.

That doesn't mean that we don't challenge each other though. We know that's a part of love as well. It seems like there are always crossroads in our journey where we must make critical decisions. Sometimes these are questions of integrity and other times they are tests to understand your commitment to a dream. The best ones – the ones that make you thankful that you have a wonderful spouse – are those where you lose sleep, take a long walk to think, or go to your knees or the prayer rug for guidance.

As I think about these crossroads for me and Christina, most of these times in our own personal journeys have revolved around some version of stepping up into a significant moment or pulling back and playing small. They revolved around taking a risk and plunging into the unknown or remaining comfortable and safe. We often chose to step into the unknown, but I can't think of a time when we made these decisions as individuals; they almost always included some nudging, encouragement and cheerleading from each other.

About five years into my teaching career, I was feeling accomplished and was getting external validation from others. I was feeling stable and safe, but Christina nudged me forward by asking if I had anything more to give and was I capable of stepping up in leadership outside of the classroom. She knew my ambitions and understood that I was choosing to play small for myself. Teaching in inner city classrooms in Philadelphia and Baltimore was amazing and transformative. It was also the opportunity to decide where my next contribution on the battlefield would be. Throughout our marriage, my wife has challenged me not to play small and to raise my eyes to the horizon, pull my shoulders back, and step up like a boss. Every once in a while, I get to do the same for her. I believe that this is about the dynamic tension between satisfaction and fear, and who knows what they look like within our spouse better than us?

In every apartment or house that we've lived, we have always considered how it will function socially. Does the space work when we have a party? Do the colors communicate both the warmth of peace and the vibrancy of this beautiful life we're creating? Likewise, we've accepted that our budget must include space for times that we will pull together to enjoy good food that someone else has cooked (i.e. "what restaurant are we going to tonight, y'all?"). We do these things because we always celebrate even the little moments of accomplishment towards the dream.

As a family, we represent many things that are not loved and honored in the world – my wife and daughter are black women, my son and I are black men, I am Muslim, we are conscious-minded and progressive politically and our heroes and sheroes all stood against the status quo. As such, we find that we have to lean into each other not only for support, but celebration. We are our own cheerleading squad, amen choir, and hype men. Our "way" has been to acknowledge and celebrate each other spontaneously and habitually. If Christina opens a new satellite office within her psychology practice, we celebrate. If I successfully accomplish one of my bucket list items, we celebrate. When our children finish a hard exam – regardless of how they did, we celebrate. Regardless of whether the feat and acknowledgements are grand or small, they are always meaningful and centered in love. This has been a beautiful and regular gift that we give to each other within our marriage. We make t-shirts, we sing to each other, we send videos and make speeches to let each other know that we see each other shining, and when one shines, so does the other.

A quarter of a century is a solid and strong measure of time. We can now measure our marriage not just in years or decades, but in fractions of centuries! It hasn't always been easy, in fact, at times it was and is challenging because we really are two perfectly imperfect people loving each other through it. I believe that we have experienced a wonderful life of supporting each other's dreams by understanding that we each are still in the process of "becoming," are consistently nudging and supporting each other and celebrating even the small victories. For us, that is the real power in this power couple.

Abdul-Malik Muhammad, Ed.D.

After the kiss,
When the fairytale dissipates
Into a lifetime of challenges,
An Imperfect union
Of marital bliss,
A forever love
With its genesis
In a simple
Trist,
The Intermingling of
I And we
Evolving into one of
God's greatest gifts,
A new life rising,
...After the kiss.

● *Coley D. Harris*

Marriage & Longevity

8

Marriage & Longevity
Melvin E. Chance

Statistic: According to the National Center for Family and Marriage Research at Bowling Green State University, only about 17 percent of married adults have been married for at least 40 years. Staying married for a lifetime is tough.

Deacon Melvin Chance and his wife Reverend Mary Ernestine Chance share the ups and downs of a marriage and factors that have allowed them to stay successfully married for 58 years.

We have been married 58 years. We have four daughters, four grandchildren, three great-grandchildren, and a host of spiritual daughters, sons and grandchildren.

How did you meet?

Melvin: One of my older cousins, who often checked on me, told me about "a nice young lady with two children," who had lost her husband. She said to me, "Why don't you settle down?" I didn't think much about it then. I went back to New York and few weeks later, I thought about that conversation. My family knew Ernestine's family. I had attended her husband's funeral. My brother knew her sister and a year later I finally got her telephone number and I called her. At the time, she was working in Connecticut. She told me she was going to stop by her aunt's house in New York on her way home to North Carolina. So, I got off work and went to her aunt's house. We met and talked for hours. We stayed in contact with each other through letters and telephone calls and that's how our romance started.

What are the most memorable moments within your Marriage?

Melvin: I was coming home to North Carolina every weekend. A carload of friends would travel from New York every weekend, so I got to see her. We started dating, and the months flew by. She was teaching at her alma mater, Conetoe High School in Conetoe, North Carolina. She was getting out of school for the summer, and I asked her to marry me. I told her if she would agree to marry me, I would ask for a week off at work. We got married on a Friday night at her mother's house. We stayed the weekend, and we went back to New York as husband and wife. So, my most memorable moment was when I asked her to marry me and she said yes! Our goal was to make the marriage work by putting God first. We went through some challenges, but there was nothing too hard for God to work out for us. First, we lived in a kitchenette in Brooklyn. Then we moved to an apartment. Then, in 1966, we were able to purchase our dream home in Queens. It seemed like God was blessing us to go forward. We lived with our four daughters in New York for 40 years. By that time, we had retired. It was an opportunity for us to return to North Carolina to help her siblings take care of their mother and father.

We start the day off in love and we end the day in love, every single day. That word love is etched in our hearts and we demonstrate it in our lives.

Talk about a challenging time and how you got through it.

Melvin: I've lost a mother, father, brother, in-laws and friends. You never get used to death. I thank God He has given us the ability to accept death. But for me, one of my most challenging times was when we were living in New York. I hoped to get a job with the City of New York because of their good retirement plan. I took the test to become a bus driver as well as several other jobs. I never got called. I remember my wife telling me, "Honey, maybe it is not God's will." I was able to get a job working in the United States Postal System, but it wasn't what I wanted to do. I wanted a better retirement plan. I kept praying to God to get it. When I first went in the postal system, they weren't paying much. We didn't start making money in the postal system until 1970, when postal workers went on strike. I was a letter carrier for 32 years. It didn't stop me from trying to apply for jobs even while I was in the postal system. But God didn't allow it. I could have had a job in sanitation, but she didn't want me to have that type of job even though it offered a better retirement plan. At one time, sanitation workers were making more than the mayor of New York City. I really wanted a better job to support my family, and just couldn't get it, but thank God for my wife, who was a teacher. We put our resources together, and we were able to live a good life and provide for our children.

The Bible says in Proverbs 31:28, "Her children arise up, and call her blessed; her husband also, and he praiseth her." How does that scripture apply to your

wife?

Melvin: I prayed to God to give me a good woman, a good wife and a mother to my children, and she is *all* of that. She is a truly a woman of God and I *truly* love her.

Why do you like opening the door for your wife?

Melvin: I feel why not? I try to show her love, true love, that agape love that I have for her. That's why I do it. It doesn't bother me at all. I did it when I was courting her. I had dated other women, but there was something about her that made her stand out from other women.

What role does God play in your marriage?

Melvin: We always put God first. If we have a misunderstanding, we sit down and talk about it. We say, let's pray about it. Let's see what God says about it. And we believe that prayer does work. The Bible says in Matthew 6:33, *"Seek ye first the kingdom of God and His righteousness and all else will be added."* We start every day with prayer. Seven days a week. We open the day with prayer and thank Him for keeping us through the day. We don't do anything without God.

What do you love about your spouse?

Melvin: First of all, I love her because she is a devoted wife.

She loves me so dearly. She is devoted to God and then she exhorts it to me. I love her because she is a devoted mother, grandmother, and great-grandmother and nurtures so many others, even if it is just a word of encouragement. She is a devoted woman of God.

What is a typical day like for you that shows your love for each other?

Melvin: My wife usually gets up about 6 a.m. and goes in the living room and she meditates for 15 or 20 minutes reading the scripture. I get up about 7 a.m. I go into meditation for a half hour, reading a daily word, and turn to a scripture in the Bible that accompanies that meditation. I read it over and over, asking God to speak to me about what the Word is saying to me that day. At 7:30 a.m., we come together and pray. We both anoint ourselves with oil, like David does in the Bible. We then get down on our knees together and start talking to God for a half hour to 45 minutes. Then we start our day. Part of our daily routine is to take our medicine. I make sure she takes her medications, which I organize for her by the week. She usually cooks breakfast for me. We also listen to gospel on various radio stations throughout the day.

When I have to go out, I say, "Honey, do you want me

to pick up anything from the store or do anything for you?" We embrace each other, we both say, "I love you," and when I return, I embrace her and let her know I'm back.

How important is communication in a marriage?
Melvin: Communication is one of the most important things in a marriage. Not just to get married and say, "Honey I love you." Communicate with each other, but most of all, talk to God. He will give you the ability to talk with each other.

You won't know how one another feels if you don't communicate with him or her or don't talk. If you just stay to yourself, you may never find out what's on each other's heart or mind. If one looks a little down, ask, "How do you feel? How are you doing? Anything bothering you?

What are some activities that you enjoy doing together?
Melvin: I enjoy being with my wife. I also like to go to a resort to get away with her for a few days and just relax. I don't think a person should always stay at home. I really enjoy being with her anywhere, though.

What message would you share with couples who aspire to have longevity in marriage?
Melvin: Don't try to do anything on your own understanding

without seeking God first. God is our refuge and strength. A very present help in trouble. When you seek God, He will lead and direct you. There are so many people who say, "Oh I'm going to do this or that," but you can do anything better when you do it with God. There were times I did not put God first, and I paid the consequences. Back then, we weren't as strong in the Word of God as we are now. That's what hindered us. In today's world, it's best to do things God's way and within His will.

As my wife said, I would suggest to any person, young or old, who is thinking about getting married, to put God first. When you don't put God first, there will be bumps that you wouldn't have had to encounter. I thank God for staying with us. I thank God for my four children. We were a happy family from day one. I didn't just marry my wife. I also married her two children. They were my children from day one. And I felt God would always be with us. I was talking with a preacher recently and he asked me, "Deacon Chance, how long have you been married?" I told him 58 years. He said, "58 years? I have a feeling God put you two together." I believe that too and I'm so glad God did.

We thank God for the cherished years of our lives together. The moments, the minutes, the hours, the years that we have been together. All the good moments outweigh the storms. We were in it together. And we thank God, that He kept us and that He is still keeping us today in love. We pray the same for you. Trust in God and put Him first. The best is yet to come!

Melvin Chance

www.ingramcontent.com/pod-product-compliance
Lightning Source LLC
Chambersburg PA
CBHW071002160426
43193CB00012B/1887